Making miniature toys and dolls

Other books by the author

Making costume dolls
Fancy dress from nursery tales
Fancy dress for girls
Presents and playthings
Gifts for the family

Making miniature toys and dolls

JEAN GREENHOWE

VNR

VAN NOSTRAND REINHOLD COMPANY
New York   Cincinnati   Toronto   London   Melbourne

Van Nostrand Reinhold Company Regional Offices:
New York   Cincinnati   Chicago   Millbrae   Dallas

Van Nostrand Reinhold Company International Offices:
London   Toronto   Melbourne

Copyright ©1977 by Jean Greenhowe
Library of Congress Catalog Card Number 77-6420
ISBN 0-442-22837-6 (hardcover)
ISBN 0-442-22838-4 (paperback)

Printed in Great Britain

First Published in Great Britain in 1977 by
B.T. Batsford Ltd.
Published in the U.S.A. in 1977 by Van Nostrand
Reinhold Company
A Division of Litton Educational Publishing, Inc.
450 West 33rd Street, New York, NY 10001

16 15 14 13 12 11 9 8 7 6 5 4 3 2 1

Library of Congress Cataloging in Publication Data

Greenhowe, Jean.
   Making miniature toys and dolls.

   1. Miniature craft.   2. Toy making.   3. Dollmaking.
I.   Title.
TT178.G73   745.59'2   77-6420
ISBN 0-442-22837-6
ISBN 0-442-22838-4 pbk.

Contents

Acknowledgment | 6
Introduction | 7

General instructions | 8
Fairy tale castles | 10
Little kitten in a mitten | 14
See-saw, Margery Daw | 16
Three felt dolls | 22
Santa Claus's special delivery | 26
Surprise clown | 31
Pixies and toadstools | 34
Two roly poly toys | 37
Six dolls in historical costume | 40
The teddy bears' picnic | 55
Four pop-up toys | 58
Mary, a miniature dressing-up doll | 63
Eight small felt animals | 76
Honey bees mobile | 80
Bean bag bunnies | 82
Bagatelle | 85
Four glove puppets – the story of the
   three little pigs | 87
Three Victorian-style dolls | 94
Magic tortoise toy | 100
Goldilocks and the three bears | 102
Punch and Judy puppet show | 112
Five fairy tale finger puppets | 114

List of stockists | 117

Acknowledgment

The designs in this book were originally featured in *Woman's Weekly* magazine and I wish to thank the editor and all staff in the home department, for their help and co-operation during the preparation of this project.

I am also indebted to Batsford for giving me the opportunity of bringing these miniature toys and dolls together in one book.

Introduction

This book contains full instructions and patterns for making dozens of miniature dolls and toys. Nursery rhymes and fairy tales are featured in the form of soft toys, finger and glove puppets, and for older children and adults instructions are given for making six peg dolls in historical dress through the ages. Also included are novelty toys such as the amusing pop-up characters, a mobile, a tiny rag doll complete with six dressing-up outfits, bean bag teddy bears with all the accessories required for their very own picnic, and lots of others too numerous to mention here.

The toys are constructed in a variety of ways, some are sewn while others are stuck together with glue. Several toys are made by an easy method I have devised when designing rather small things whereby the toy is cut out *after* it has been stitched. This makes the accurate seaming of tiny pieces of fabric a simple matter. Only small amounts of fabrics and trimmings are required for making the toys and dolls, plus discarded household odds and ends. All the patterns are printed full size among the instructions for each item, and may be traced directly off the pages.

General instructions

Materials

Many of the materials required are household items such as matchboxes, washing-up liquid bottles and cardboard tubes. These tubes, from the centre of toilet rolls or paper towels, are usually of standard size measuring about 4 cm ($1\frac{1}{2}$ in.) in diameter.

Cuttings of old nylon tights and stockings are used for some of the toys and these should be about 20 or 30 denier and in the normal brown shades.

Pink stockinette for doll making can sometimes be difficult to obtain. In this case a plain cotton vest or T-shirt tinted with flesh-coloured dye serves exactly the same purpose.

Synthetic foam bath sponge is very good for making small bushes and shrubs on model toys and if green is unobtainable a yellow sponge can be dyed most successfully.

For stuffing toys, kapok or cotton wool can be used or man-made fibre stuffing if the toy is to be washable. Foam chip stuffing is unsuitable for very small toys as it is far too lumpy.

When black felt is required, for example for the eyes on soft toys and dolls, black interlining can be used instead as this cuts very evenly. A small piece can be kept handy just for toymaking.

Scraps of fabrics from the rag bag, dressmaking cuttings, felt and trimmings of all kinds should of course be saved up for toymaking. Most of the other materials required are easily obtainable but in case of difficulty a list of possible suppliers is given at the back of the book.

Gluing

When adhesive is quoted in the instructions it should be a quick drying all-purpose glue such as UHU, Unwanted smears of such glue are easily removed from fabrics by dabbing *carefully* with a little acetone.

Raw edges of woven fabrics can be sealed to prevent fraying by spreading a little glue on the wrong side.

When cutting out tiny pieces of felt it is sometimes difficult to get neat even shapes as the cut edges of the felt tend to be somewhat fluffy. To remedy this, first coat the wrong side of the felt with glue and allow it to dry before cutting out the pieces.

Note that the large size tube of this kind of glue is usually sold complete with a narrow plastic screw-on nozzle, and this simplifies the application of tiny dabs of glue.

Patterns, sewing and cutting out

The pattern shapes are printed full size. They can be traced off the page using thin writing paper then all printed details should be marked onto each piece. Some patterns are simply rectangles, squares or circles and the sizes for these are given in the instructions. They should be drawn out using a ruler or compasses.

Some of the toys are made by what I call the 'stitch-around' method (see diagram 1). For these the patterns are traced off the page, cut out, then pinned onto two layers of fabric. The fabric is then machine stitched through both layers all round the edge of the paper pattern, following the shape of the pattern closely, and leaving a gap in the stitching as shown in the diagram. After removing the pattern the toy is cut out close to the stitching line and then usually it is stuffed without turning if made from felt. If woven or knitted fabric has been used, the toy is turned right side out before stuffing.

All fabric pieces should be joined having the right sides of the fabric together unless otherwise stated in the instructions.

After sewing seams in fur fabric or fleece, pick out the pile trapped in the seam on the right side of the fabric using the point of a pin or needle.

When embroidering facial features on a doll or toy, start and fasten off the threads in a position where they will be hidden on the finished toy, for example underneath a felt nose or eye, behind the hairline or at the back of the head.

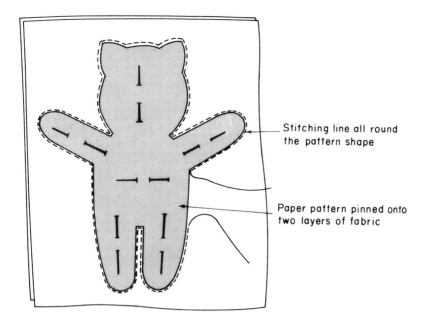

Stitching line all round
the pattern shape

Paper pattern pinned onto
two layers of fabric

DIAGRAM 1

The stitch-around method of
sewing toys

Before cutting out cotton stockinette be sure to test the fabric by pulling, to find the direction in which the fabric stretches most. Patterns should then be pinned onto the fabric having the 'most stretch' in the direction shown on each pattern piece.

Safety in toys
When making any toy for a particular child it is important to consider the safety factor in exactly the same way as when buying toys. Care should be taken to make sure that the toy is suitable for the child's age group. Very young children in particular should not be given toys containing wire, buttons, beads or other items which could be detached and swallowed.

Metric and imperial measurements
All sizes in this book have been worked out in both metric and imperial so that in many instances the measurements given are not absolutely accurate conversions. This has been done to avoid having awkward sizes where in fact a little extra either way makes no difference to the appearance of the finished toy. The toy maker can use either metric or imperial as desired.

Fairy tale castles

Figure 1 Fairy tale castles

These pretty model castles measure 11.5 cm (4½ in.) and 20.5 cm (8 in.) in height (fig. 1). They are made from tubes of card covered with fabric. Narrow strips of leather, snipped along one edge to make a fringe, are used for covering the pointed roofs to give the effect of roof tiles.

Materials required

Scraps of fabrics, braid, trimmings, leather, felt and
    green synthetic foam sponge
Cardboard tubes and card
Two matchsticks and two small beads
Black marker pen
Kapok, cotton wool or man-made fibre stuffing
Adhesive

To make the small castle

Cut the small castle base from green fabric using pattern 1a, and mark the dotted dart lines on the wrong side of the fabric. Fold each dart along the fold line and stitch through the dotted lines. Cut a circle of card to the size shown at the centre of the castle base pattern. Stick the card circle to the centre of the base on the wrong side of the fabric. Turn in the outer raw edge of the fabric circle 6 mm (¼ in.) and run a strong gathering thread round it but do not pull up the gathers just yet.

The towers on the castle are made by cutting cardboard tubes along the length then lapping the cut edges and gluing to give the required diameter. For the main tower make a tube measuring 2 cm (¾ in.) diameter by 5.5 cm (2¼ in.) long. Cover the tower by gluing on a strip of fabric, turning the raw edges of the fabric in over the ends of the tube to neaten. For the top tower make a tube measuring 1.6 cm (⅝ in.) diameter by 2.5 cm (1 in.) long. Cover the tube with fabric, then glue it just inside one end of the main tower.

For the pointed roof, cut the roof from paper using pattern 1b, placing the edge of the pattern indicated against a fold in the paper. Bend and glue this semi-circle into a cone shape to fit over the top tower. For the roof tiles cut 6 mm (¼ in.) wide strips of leather then snip all along one long edge at about 3 mm (⅛ in.) intervals. Now starting at the lower edge of the roof, glue the strips round and round in a spiral until the roof is completely covered.

For the flag, pare down a matchstick then glue a short length of braid or ribbon round one end. Pierce a hole on the top of the roof with the point of the scissors then glue the matchstick into it. Stick a small bead on the top of the matchstick then trim the end of the flag to a V-shape as illustrated.

For the small tower at the side of the castle, roll up a small strip of fabric spread with glue to make the tower about 1 cm (⅜ in.) diameter by 2 cm (¾ in.) long. Cut and make the roof of the tower from paper as for the castle tower using pattern 1c. Cover the roof by gluing on a piece of leather cut to shape. Glue the tower to one side of the main tower as shown in the illustration holding it in position with pins until the glue is dry.

To assemble the fabric base and castle, spread glue on the lower edge of the main tower and place it in the centre of the cardboard circle which is glued to the fabric base. Allow the glue to dry, then stuff the base pulling up the gathering thread at the same time until the gathered edge fits tightly round the main tower. Fasten off the gathering thread.

For the door, cut a piece of leather measuring 1.3 cm by 2 cm (½ in. by ¾ in.), glue it in place on the main tower, then glue on a bit of braid around the door for the door frame as illustrated. Mark hinges and a door knob on the door using black marker pen. Snip a narrow strip of leather along one edge and glue it around the top of the main tower for the battlements as illustrated.

Glue on a strip of braid for a pathway winding down from the door to the lower edge of the base. Glue bits of green sponge here and there on the base for bushes.

Cut pieces of black felt for the windows measuring about 6 mm by 9 mm (¼ in. by ⅜ in.). Round off the top corners and glue the windows to the castle towers as illustrated. Mark stones around each window and on the walls here and there using a black marker pen.

To make the large castle

Make in the same basic way as the small castle using the following sizes. Use patterns 1d and 1e for the base and roof of the large castle; for the main tower make a tube 3 cm (1¼ in.) diameter by 7.5 cm (3 in.) long, for the middle tower, a tube 2.5 cm (1 in.) diameter by 4 cm (1½ in.) long, and for the top tower a tube 2 cm (¾ in.) diameter by 2.5 cm (1 in.) long.

Cut a piece of leather for the door measuring 1.6 cm by 2.5 cm (⅝ in. by 1 in.). Make one side tower the same size as that used for the small castle, and make the second side tower a little larger.

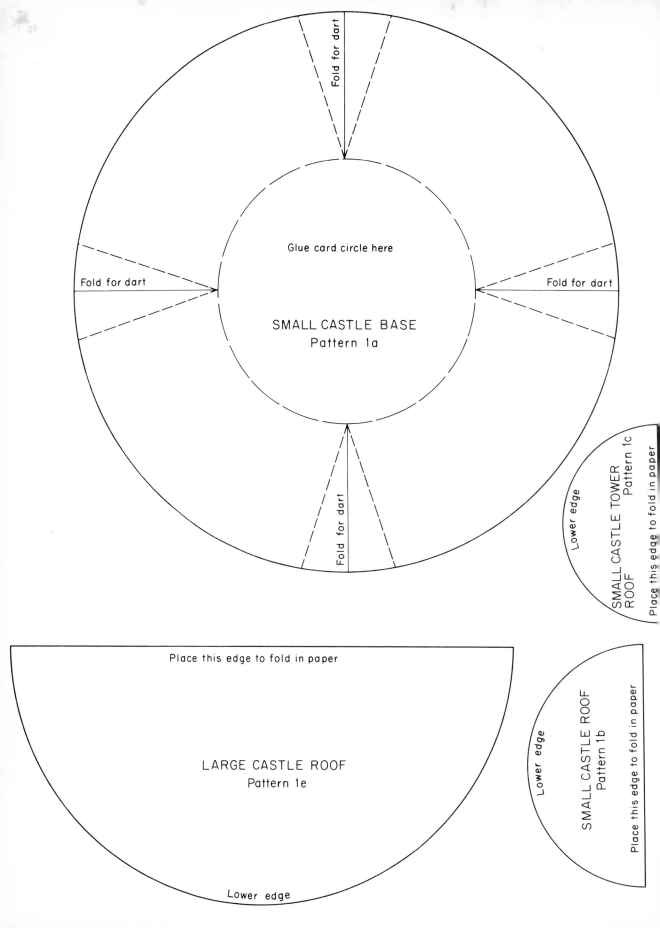

Fold for dart

Fold for dart

Fold for dart

Fold for dart

Glue card circle here

SMALL CASTLE BASE
Pattern 1a

SMALL CASTLE TOWER
ROOF Pattern 1c

Lower edge

Place this edge to fold in paper

Place this edge to fold in paper

LARGE CASTLE ROOF
Pattern 1e

Lower edge

SMALL CASTLE ROOF
Pattern 1b

Lower edge

Place this edge to fold in paper

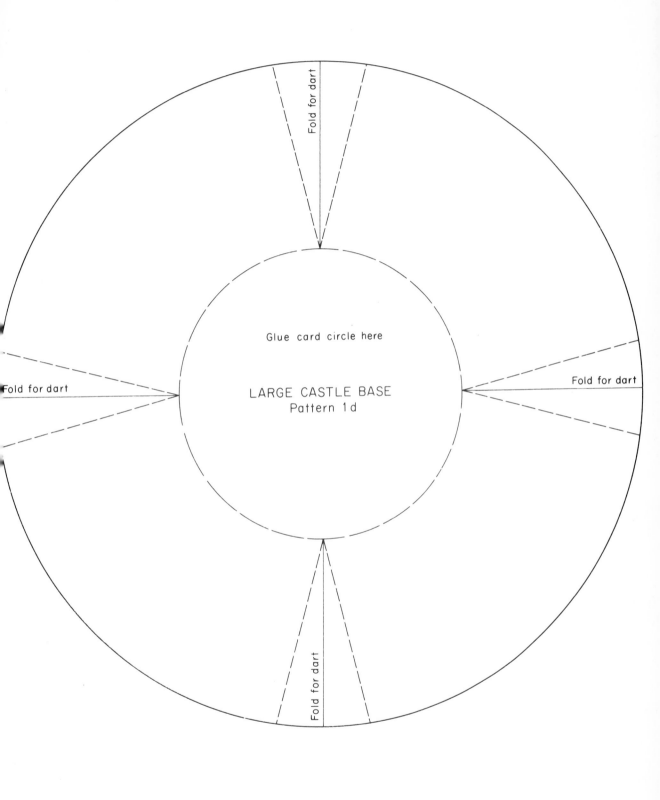

Fold for dart

Glue card circle here

LARGE CASTLE BASE
Pattern 1d

Fold for dart

Fold for dart

Fold for dart

Little kitten in a mitten

Figure 2 Little kitten in a mitten

LITTLE KITTEN
Pattern 2a

Leave open

The kitten stuffed felt toy measures just 10 cm (4 in.) in height and he fits snugly inside his own little fabric mitten (fig. 2). The mitten can be sewn onto a child's T-shirt or jeans if desired, like a pocket, then the toy can be popped inside. Another idea would be to make three little kittens in mittens to represent the popular nursery rhyme. The kitten is made by the stitch-around method and the toy is stuffed before cutting out. All seams and turnings are given in the instructions.

Materials required
Scraps of felt, fabric, ribbon, trimming and stuffing
Red and black thread for the facial features
Adhesive

To make the kitten
Trace the kitten pattern 2a off the page onto thin paper. Pin the paper pattern onto two layers of felt then machine stitch all round close to the edge of the paper pattern, leaving a gap in the stitching as indicated on the pattern. Now take the felt pieces off the machine and remove the paper pattern. Push a little stuffing inside the stitched kitten shape, spread it out evenly and push it into the legs and arms with a knitting needle. Machine stitch the gap left in the stitching, knot all the thread ends then sew them into the kitten's body.

Cut out the kitten close to the stitching line. Work the mouth and nose in red thread and the whiskers in black thread as shown on the pattern. Cut circles of black felt for the eyes to the size shown then glue them in place. Tie a bow of narrow ribbon round the kitten's neck.

To make the mitten
Cut one pair of mitten pieces from fabric using pattern 2b. Join the pieces taking a 6 mm ($\frac{1}{4}$ in.) seam and leaving the upper edges open as shown on the pattern. Trim the seam and clip round the curves then turn the mitten right side out and press. Make a narrow hem round the upper edges and sew on the trimming.

Upper edge leave open

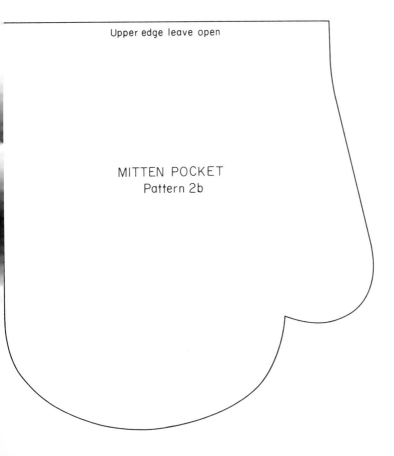

MITTEN POCKET
Pattern 2b

15

See-saw, Margery Daw

16

Here is a different version of a 'swinging weight' toy (see colour plate 1). Usually this type of toy depicts three wooden chickens on a board. From each one a string passes through the board and is attached to a weight underneath. As the weight is set revolving, the chickens peck at the board in rotation. In the toy illustrated (fig. 3) the weight sets the see-saw in motion. The base measures about 18 cm by 23 cm (7 in. by 9 in.) including the handle. Wooden balls or beads measuring 2 cm ($\frac{3}{4}$ in.) diameter are used for the heads of the little figures and pipe cleaners are used for the bodies. The only other materials required are scraps of fabric, trimmings and card. The garments on the figures are made from squares or rectangles of fabric and all raw edges are turned in or overlapped 3 mm ($\frac{1}{8}$ in.) unless otherwise stated.

Materials required for the base

Corrugated reinforced cardboard (cut from a grocery box)

Strip of 3 mm ($\frac{1}{8}$ in.) thick plywood for the see-saw, or layers of thin card can be glued together instead of using wood

Thin cord or string and a ball or bead about 2.5 cm (1 in.) diameter for the weight

Braid, 90 cm (1 yd) of 1.3 cm ($\frac{1}{2}$ in.) wide

Small pieces of green and brown fabric or felt

Bits of green synthetic foam sponge

Small guipure flowers or dried flowers

A cardboard tube and thin card

Adhesive

To make the base

Trace the base pattern 3a off the page onto thin paper. Draw round this paper shape four times onto the reinforced cardboard changing the direction of the pattern each time so that the corrugated reinforcing will lie in a different direction (this is to strengthen the base). Cut out, then glue all the base pieces together. Pierce the two see-saw holes carefully through the base at the positions shown on the pattern, first by using the point of the scissors then by pushing a pencil right through to enlarge the holes.

Cut two pieces of green fabric 3 mm ($\frac{1}{8}$ in.) larger all round than the base pattern. Snip small holes in each piece at the positions of the see-saw holes in the base. Glue one fabric piece in position on the base turning and sticking the 3 mm ($\frac{1}{8}$ in.) extra onto the

sides of the base all round. Push the raw edges of the fabric at the see-saw holes right into the holes using a little glue to neaten the raw edges and hold them in place. Glue the other fabric piece to the underside of the base in the same way. Glue braid all round the sides of the base to cover the raw edges of the green fabric.

For the log on which the see-saw is balanced, cut a 5 cm (2 in.) section off the cardboard tube. Cut this section along the length then overlap and glue the cut edges to make a 2.5 cm (1 in.) diameter tube. To each end of the log glue a 2.5 cm (1 in.) diameter circle of card marked into 'growth' rings as illustrated. Glue a strip of brown fabric or felt round the log for the bark. Stick the log in the position shown on the base pattern, first spreading the surface of the base and log with glue and allowing it to dry before once more coating with glue and sticking in place. Arrange bits of green foam sponge and flowers round the log as illustrated, and glue them in position.

Cut out the see-saw to the size shown in pattern 3b. Bore a hole large enough for the string or cord to pass through, in each end of the see-saw at the positions shown on the pattern. Mark the centre line on the see-saw, then for the 'hinge' pieces cut two 1.3 cm by 2.5 cm ($\frac{1}{2}$ in. by 1 in.) strips of fabric. Fold each strip in half bringing the short edges together. Glue half of each strip in position on either side of the centre of the see-saw, leaving the other halves free as shown on the see-saw pattern. Allow the glue to dry, then spread the remaining halves of the hinge pieces with glue, and place the see-saw centrally on the log, holding the hinges in position on the log with pins until the glue dries. Work the see-saw back and forth to see that it moves quite freely and is properly balanced.

Cut two 30.5 cm (12 in.) lengths of cord or string and one 28 cm (11 in.) length. Make a small knot in one end of each string. Thread the 30.5 cm (12 in.) lengths through the holes in the see-saw then through the holes in the base. Using a darning needle, take the 28 cm (11 in.) length of cord through the base at the position shown on the base pattern. Bring all the cords together underneath the base with the ends level. Knot them together 13 cm (5 in.) from the ends. Thread the remaining three ends through the bead weight, and knot them. If a wooden ball with a hole bored only part of the way through is used for the weight, tie the ends of the cord into a large knot and glue the knot into the hole in the ball.

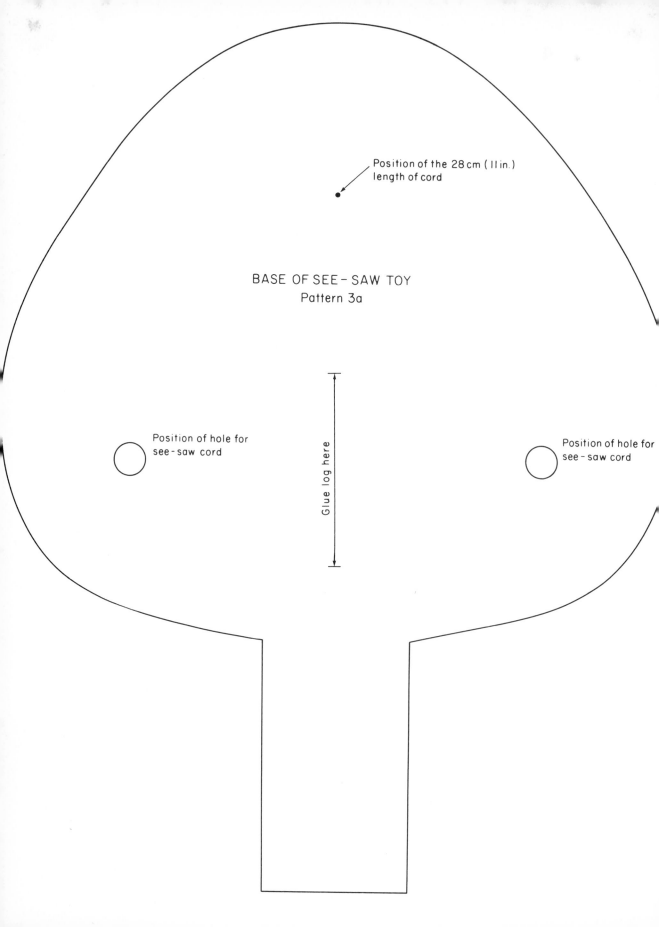

Position of the 28 cm (11 in.)
length of cord

BASE OF SEE – SAW TOY
Pattern 3a

Position of hole for
see – saw cord

Glue log here

Position of hole for
see – saw cord

Materials required for each of the figures

Three pipe cleaners
A wooden ball or bead 2 cm ($\frac{3}{4}$ in.) in diameter
Cotton wool
Scraps of fabric, felt, trimming, ribbon and cuttings
    off nylon stockings or tights
Embroidery thread for the hair
Pencils and pens for colouring the face
Adhesive

To make the basic figure

For each arm cut a 6.5 cm ($2\frac{1}{2}$ in.) length of pipe cleaner. For each leg cut a 10 cm (4 in.) length of pipe cleaner. Glue one end of each, 6 mm ($\frac{1}{4}$ in.) into the ball. Twist the leg pipe cleaners together for 2.5 cm (1 in.) forming the body, then fold 1.3 cm ($\frac{1}{2}$ in.) round at the ends for the feet and turn these up (see diagram 2). Fold the ends of the arms round 1.3 cm ($\frac{1}{2}$ in.) for the hands. Cut a 2.5 cm (1 in.) diameter circle of nylon stocking or tights fabric, place the end of one hand in the centre then draw back the edges of the circle towards the arm. Tie sewing thread round the wrist to hold the fabric in place then trim off the excess fabric. Cover the other hand in the same way. Wrap a little cotton wool around the body and each limb to pad out slightly.

Cut four shoe pieces from felt using pattern 3c, then cut a slit in two of the pieces as shown by the dotted line on the pattern. Glue the shoe pieces in pairs to each foot, having the slit pieces as the shoe uppers, and taking the felt on either side of the slit round the pipe cleaner leg towards the back of the foot.

Mark on the face using an ordinary pencil, then colour the cheeks with red pencil and the eyes with black pen.

To make the girl

For the hair, wind embroidery thread six times around three fingers. Slip this small hank off the fingers and tie at the centre with a strand of thread. Glue this tied centre to the top of the girl's head and the looped ends down each side of the face then towards the back of the head.

For each pants leg cut a 4 cm ($1\frac{1}{2}$ in.) square of fabric. Glue lace trimming to one edge of each square for the lower edge of the pants. Place one around each leg overlapping and gluing the edges.

For the dress bodice cut a 2.5 cm by 5.5 cm (1 in. by $2\frac{1}{4}$ in.) strip of fabric. Spread it with glue and stick it around the figure beneath the arms having the upper edge as close to the neck as possible and overlapping and gluing the 2.5 cm (1 in.) edges at the back of the figure. To neaten the neck edge at the front of the bodice, cut the girl's bodice front piece from two layers of fabric stuck together, using pattern 3d. Stick the bodice front piece in place.

For each sleeve cut a 3 cm by 4 cm ($1\frac{1}{4}$ in. by $1\frac{1}{2}$ in.) piece of fabric then overlap and glue the 3 cm ($1\frac{1}{4}$ in.) edges. Slip a sleeve over each arm then run gathering threads round the raw edges and pull them up and fasten off at the wrists and shoulders. Stick a scrap of lace trimming round each wrist to cover the raw edges. For the lace collar cut two 10 cm (4 in.) lengths of 1.3 cm ($\frac{1}{2}$ in.) wide lace edging. Place them together and gather along one edge through both thicknesses pulling up the gathers to measure 7.5 cm (3 in.). Glue the collar round the back of the neck and down each side of the bodice as illustrated.

For the dress skirt cut a 4 cm by 13 cm ($1\frac{1}{2}$ in. by 5 in.) strip of fabric. Turn in one 13 cm (5 in.) edge and glue, for the hem. Overlap and glue the short edges. Gather the remaining raw edge and place the skirt on the figure. Pull up the gathers round the waist and fasten off. Stick a length of narrow ribbon, for a sash, round the waist to cover the raw edges. Stick a small ribbon bow to the back of the sash.

For the hat cut a 4.5 cm by 13 cm ($1\frac{3}{4}$ in. by 5 in.) strip of fabric. Overlap and stick the short edges. With the wrong side of the hat outside, gather up one 13 cm (5 in.) edge tightly and fasten off. Turn back the remaining raw edge 6 mm ($\frac{1}{4}$ in.) and run a gathering thread through both thicknesses near the raw edge. Turn the hat right side out and place on the girl's head, pulling up and fastening off the gathering thread to fit. Stuff a little cotton wool in the top of the hat to shape it, then glue the hat to the head. Glue a strip of narrow ribbon round the gathered part of the hat.

To make the boy

Make the boy's hair as for the girl's but wind the thread around two fingers and tie a thread round the hank off centre for a 'side parting' effect.

Make the pants as for the girl's, omitting the lace trimming, and instead turning in and sticking the lower edges to neaten.

For each sleeve of the boy's smock cut a 4.5 cm by 5 cm ($1\frac{3}{4}$ in. by 2 in.) piece of fabric. Turn in 6 mm ($\frac{1}{4}$ in.) at one 4.5 cm ($1\frac{3}{4}$ in.) edge of each piece, and run a gathering thread round to fit the wrists. Place a sleeve on each arm and overlap and

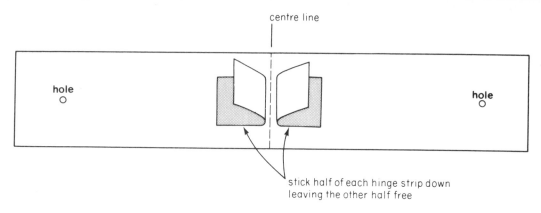

centre line

hole
○

hole
○

stick half of each hinge strip down
leaving the other half free

Pattern 3b   THE SEE-SAW

neck edge

Pattern 3d
GIRL'S BODICE
FRONT PIECE

cut slit here

Pattern 3c
SHOE

Pattern 3e
BOY'S COLLAR

Pattern 3f
BOY'S CAP PEAK

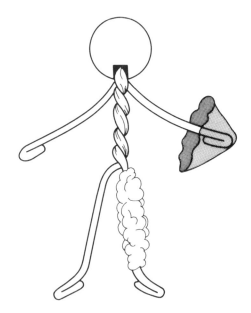

DIAGRAM 2   How to make the basic figure

stick the 5 cm (2 in.) edges. Gather the upper edges and stick to the shoulders.

For the front and back of the smock cut two 4.5 cm by 6.5 cm (1¾ in. by 2½ in.) pieces of fabric. Turn in and stick the edges of each piece except for one 6.5 cm (2½ in.) edge which will be the neck edge. Run three gathering threads across each piece, one close to the neck edge and the other two at 6 mm (¼ in.) intervals further down, pull up the gathers to measure 2.5 cm (1 in.), and fasten off. Stick the front and back of the smock in place, lapping the side edges over the top raw edges of the sleeves, then lapping the remainder of the sides over each other underneath the boy's arms.

For the collar stick two layers of fabric together, then when the glue is dry cut out the collar using pattern 3e. Glue the collar round the boy's neck.

For the hat band, stick a length of 6 mm (¼ in.) wide tape, ribbon or felt round the boy's head from the top round to the back of the neck. Glue together two bits of tape, then from this cut out the cap peak using pattern 3f. Glue the straight edge of the peak to the hat band at the front. For the top of the hat cut a 4 cm (1½ in.) diameter circle of felt. Run a gathering thread round, close to the edge of the circle, then place the gathered edge over the hat band pulling up the gathers to fit. Fasten off, then glue the top of the hat to the head, lapping it about 3 mm (⅛ in.) over the hat band.

To position the figures on the base

Bend the boy and girl to sit on each end of the see-saw, then glue them in position, sticking one hand of each to the see-saw as illustrated. Make another figure, either a boy or a girl, and stick it in place at the back of the base as shown in the illustration. Stick a few more bits of green sponge and flowers to the base on either side of the third figure.

Three felt dolls, Bo-Peep, Red Riding Hood and Miss Muffet

Figure 4 Three felt dolls: Bo-Peep, Little Miss Muffet, Red Riding Hood

These nursery-tale dolls measure about 24 cm (9½ in.) in height (fig. 4). They are all very quick to make from the same basic one-piece pattern using the stitch-around method. All the clothes are made from strips or circles of fabric and they are stuck or sewn directly onto the dolls. Turnings and seams of 6 mm (¼ in.) are allowed on all the clothes. On the doll pattern, the outline is the actual stitching line.

Materials required

Two pieces of pink felt, 20 cm × 26 cm (8 in. × 10¼ in.), for each doll
Kapok, cotton wool or man-made fibre stuffing
Scraps of fabrics, trimmings, ribbon and black felt
Pink lipstick for colouring the cheeks
Oddments of 4-ply knitting wool or yarn for the hair
One pipe cleaner and an equal length of shoe lace for Bo-Peep's crook
A few dried flowers for Red Riding Hood
Small safety pins (optional)
Adhesive

To make the basic doll

Trace the doll pattern 4a off the page onto a piece of thin paper. Cut out the pattern, then pin it onto two layers of felt. Machine stitch all round close to the edge of the paper pattern, leaving a gap in the stitching at the top of the doll's head as indicated on the pattern. Remove the paper pattern and cut out the doll close to the stitching all round.

Stuff the doll through the head, pushing the stuffing in with a knitting needle. Stuff the legs first, then the arms, then the body, and finally the head. Tie two strands of sewing thread fairly tightly around the neck, taking care not to pucker the felt. Sew the thread ends into the neck.

For the eyes cut two circles of black felt to the size shown on the pattern. Stick them in place on the face. Colour the cheeks by rubbing in a little lipstick. For the hair, make a hank of wool or yarn by winding it sixteen times around a 25 cm (10 in.) length of card. Slip the hank off the card and tie a strand of wool around the centre of the hank. Sew this tied centre to the forehead at the position shown on the pattern. Take the wool strands to each side of the head and sew in position in a bunch letting the looped ends of the wool hang down.

To make Miss Muffet

To complete the hair, cut through the looped ends of the wool strands then trim them to an even length.

For the dress bodice cut two 7 cm (2¾ in.) squares of fabric. Turn in all the raw edges of each piece and stick down to neaten. Glue one square to the front of the doll beneath the chin and glue the other square to the back in the same way, so that two corners of each square will meet on the shoulders. Glue a small ribbon bow to the bodice front at the neck edge.

For the skirt cut a 9 cm by 28 cm (3½ in. by 11 in.) strip of fabric, and for the frill cut a 5 cm by 50 cm (2 in. by 20 in.) strip. Make a narrow hem on one long raw edge of the frill strip, gather the remaining long raw edge to fit one long edge of the skirt strip then sew it in place. Join the short edges of the skirt and frill. Turn in the remaining raw edge of the skirt and run round a gathering thread. Put the skirt on the doll then pull up the gathers tightly beneath the doll's arms and fasten off. Space out the gathers evenly all round, then sew the gathered edge of the skirt to the doll.

For the shawl cut an 18 cm (7 in.) square of fabric and fray out all the raw edges. Fold the shawl corner to corner, and place it around the doll, turning over the folded edge about 2 cm (¾ in.). Secure the ends of the shawl at the centre front with a small safety pin or sew in place if desired.

For the hat cut two 18 cm (7 in.) diameter circles from net or other non-fray fabric. Place the circles together and run a gathering thread round them about 2 cm (¾ in.) from the raw edges. Place the hat on the doll's head and pull up the gathers to fit so that the hat covers all of the head except for the hair at the front. Fasten off the gathers then catch the hat to the head through the gathers all round. Tie a length of ribbon round the gathers knotting it at the front of the hat.

For the spider cut a 2 cm (¾ in.) diameter circle of black felt. Run a gathering thread round the edge then put a little bit of stuffing in the centre of the felt, pull up the gathers and fasten off. Use black thread for the spider's legs. Take stitches through the body leaving loops of thread at each side and over-sewing each time to secure the loops. Cut through the thread loops and trim the legs to an even length. Work eyes on the spider with a few small stitches using white thread. Suspend the spider from Miss Muffet's hat with a length of white thread as shown in the illustration.

To make Red Riding Hood

Before sewing the hank of wool to the head, sew a few small loops of wool to the forehead to hang down for a fringe. Do not cut the looped ends of the hank

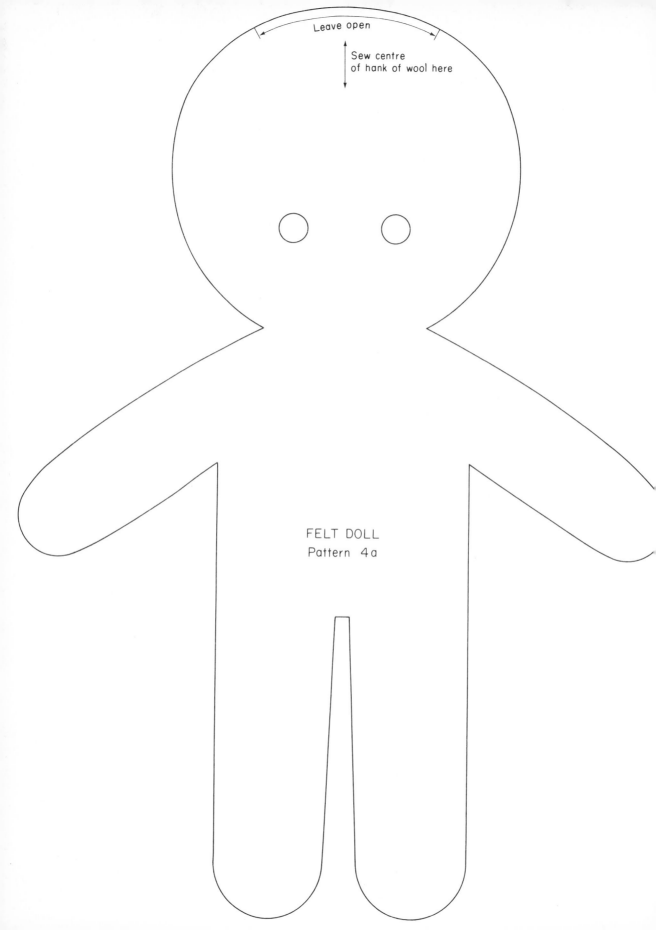

Leave open

Sew centre
of hank of wool here

FELT DOLL
Pattern 4a

of wool but take them toward the back of the head and sew in place.

For the blouse glue a 6 cm (2⅜ in.) square of trimming or ribbon to the front and back of the doll.

For the skirt cut a 13 cm by 28 cm (5 in. by 11 in.) strip of fabric. Hem one long edge of the strip then sew on ric-rac braid or other trimming as shown in the illustration. Join the short edges of the skirt strip then turn in and gather the remaining raw edge, fitting it onto the doll in the same way as for Miss Muffet. Tie a length of ribbon or tape for a sash around the gathered edge, knotting it at the centre front. Cut a 14 cm (5½ in.) square of fabric to match the skirt and fray out the raw edges a little. Fold the square corner to corner, then turn over the folded edge and place around the doll's neck, tucking the corners into the sash at the front as shown in the illustration.

For the hood, cut a 20 cm (8 in.) square of red fabric. Fray out the raw edges a little then fold the square corner to corner. Place around the doll's head overlapping all the corners at the back and pinning them in place with a small safety pin. Alternatively, sew the corners in place.

Cut two basket pieces from fabric using pattern 4b. Join the pieces round the curved edges taking a narrow seam, turn right side out then turn in and stick down the top raw edges to neaten. Make a narrow handle from a strip of fabric. Stick the ends of the handle to the basket then sew the handle to Red Riding Hood's arm as shown in the illustration. Glue a bit of fabric and a few dried flowers inside the basket.

To make Bo-Peep

Make the hair in the same way as for Red Riding Hood, omitting the fringe. Make the bodice in the same way as for Miss Muffet, and the skirt as for Red Riding Hood. Glue trimming to the armhole edges of the bodice and around the top gathered edge of the skirt and also the hem edge. Sew a ribbon bow to the front neck edge of the bodice.

For the hat cut a 20 cm by 50 cm (8 in. by 20 in.) strip of fabric. Join the short edges of the strip. Fold the strip in half along the length right side out, bringing the raw edges together. Run a gathering thread round the raw edges, pull up the gathers tightly and fasten off. Turn the hat right side out. Run round a gathering thread 2 cm (¾ in.) from the folded edge. Place the hat on the doll's head, pull up the gathers to fit, and sew the hat in place in the same way as for Miss Muffet's hat. Glue trimming round the hat gathers.

For the crook, push the pipe cleaner inside an equal length of shoe lace. Stick the ends of the shoe lace to the pipe cleaner. Bend to form a crook shape then tie on a ribbon bow and sew the crook to the doll's arm.

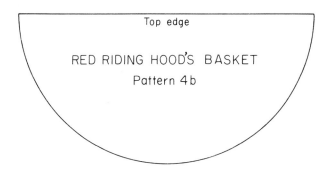

RED RIDING HOOD'S BASKET
Pattern 4b
Top edge

Santa Claus's special delivery

Figure 5 Santa Claus's special delivery

Instead of the usual advent calender for counting the days to Christmas, here is a novel advent toy (fig. 5). There are twenty-five parcels in Santa's sack, one for every day in December up to Christmas day. The tiny parcels contain small sweets, tiny plastic toys or lucky charms and each parcel is numbered. Alternatively the toy could be used as a table centre piece at a children's party with a parcel for every child in the sack, each one marked with a child's name. The snow covered base, which represents a roof-top complete with chimneys, measures 25.5 cm by 33 cm (10 in. by 13 in.). Santa is about 25.5 cm (10 in.) in height and his reindeer measures 18 cm (7 in.). All are easy to make from household odds and ends and throw-away packages.

Materials required for the base and chimney

Cardboard (cut from a grocery box) for the base
Small roll of cotton wool, for the snow
Cardboard carton measuring about 5 cm × 10 cm × 11.5 cm (2 in. × 4 in. × 4½ in.) for the chimney
Brick-effect paper or red paper
Cardboard tube about 4 cm (1½ in.) in diameter for the chimney pots
Black shoe lace and four pipe cleaners for the TV aerial
Red and black paint or marker pens
Adhesive

To make the base and chimney

Cut a 25.5 cm by 33 cm (10 in. by 13 in.) piece of cardboard for the base. Cover it by sticking on cotton wool wound off the roll.

Take the cardboard carton for the chimney and cover it with brick effect paper, or stick on red paper and then mark it into bricks all over. For each chimney pot cut a 4 cm (1½ in.) long section off the cardboard tube. Colour the chimneys black inside and red outside, then glue them in position side by side on top of the brick chimney. Stick a strip of black shoe lace round the top of each chimney pot. Glue bits of cotton wool on the top of the chimney for snow. Glue the chimney in position on the base as shown in the illustration, clearing away the cotton wool underneath it so that the chimney will stick properly.

For the cross bar of the TV aerial cut a 7.5 cm (3 in.) length of pipe cleaner. Cut two 13 cm (5 in.) lengths of pipe cleaner for the side pieces. Use a full length pipe cleaner for the central pole which will be fixed onto the chimney. Push each length of pipe cleaner inside an equal length of black shoe lace. Seal all the cut ends of the shoe lace over the ends of the pipe cleaners by spreading on a little glue and pressing the cut ends together. Assemble the aerial as illustrated bending the gluing 6 mm (¼ in.) at each end of the cross bar round the side pieces. Bend and glue 6 mm (¼ in.) at one end of the central pole round the cross bar. Glue the other end of the central pole down the back of the chimney. Glue bits of cotton wool to the cross bar for snow.

Materials required for Santa Claus

A plastic washing-up liquid container about 6.5 cm (2½ in.) in diameter
Scraps of white fleecy fabric for edging the clothes
Scraps of white long pile fur fabric for the beard and hair
Red velvet or cloth for the gown and cap
Scraps of pink, black and red felt
28 cm (11 in.) length of ribbon for the belt and a buckle to fit the ribbon width
Cotton wool for stuffing

To make Santa Claus

Cut the top off the plastic bottle so that the remaining portion is 19 cm (7½ in.) in height. For the gown cut a 19 cm by 25.5 cm (7½ in. by 10 in.) strip of red fabric. Glue a 1.3 cm (½ in.) wide strip of white fleecy fabric to one 25.5 cm (10 in.) raw edge. Overlap the 19 cm (7½ in.) edges a little and stick; note that this join should be at the back of Santa Claus when sticking on the face etc. Place the gown over the bottle having the upper raw edge even with the top edge of the bottle. Glue this edge in place easing the fabric into creases as necessary, to fit.

Cut the face piece from pink felt using pattern 5a. Glue it to the gown at the front of the figure having the upper edge even with the top of the bottle as indicated. Cut the beard from long-pile white fur fabric, having the pile of the fabric in the direction shown on pattern 5b and snipping through the back of the fabric only, so as not to cut through the long fur pile. Glue the beard in place as shown on the face pattern (5a). Cut out the eyes from black felt, the nose from red felt, and for the eyebrows use cuttings of white fur fabric. Glue them all in place. Cut a narrow strip of fur fabric for a mustache and stick in place as illustrated, smoothing it into shape by spreading the centre and ends with glue.

For the belt, fix the buckle to one end of the ribbon, place around Santa's waist, and fasten the other end of the ribbon through the buckle.

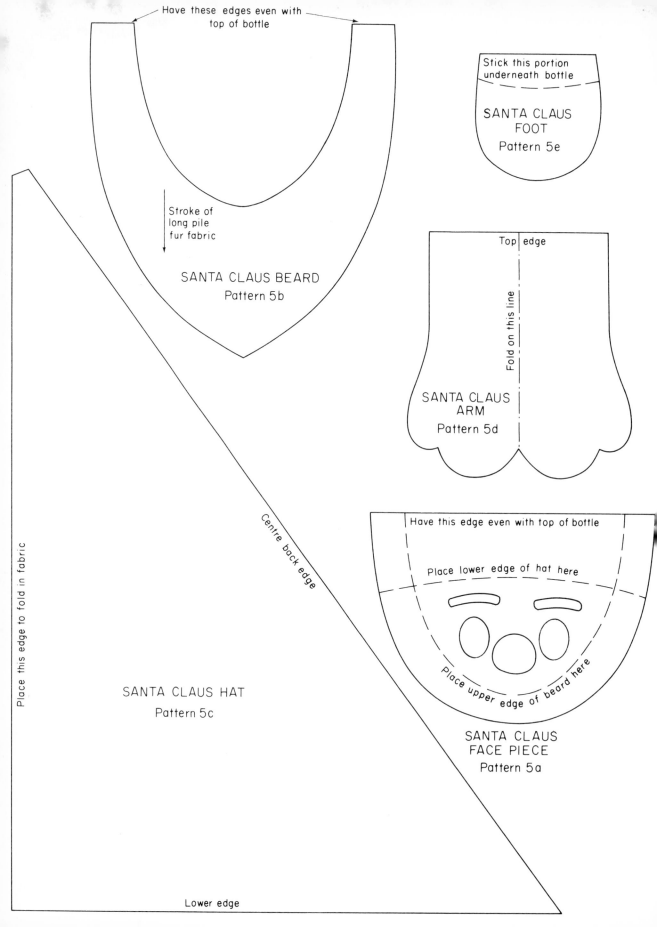

Have these edges even with top of bottle

Stroke of long pile fur fabric

SANTA CLAUS BEARD
Pattern 5b

Place this edge to fold in fabric

Centre back edge

SANTA CLAUS HAT
Pattern 5c

Lower edge

Stick this portion underneath bottle

SANTA CLAUS FOOT
Pattern 5e

Top edge

Fold on this line

SANTA CLAUS ARM
Pattern 5d

Have this edge even with top of bottle

Place lower edge of hat here

Place upper edge of beard here

SANTA CLAUS FACE PIECE
Pattern 5a

Cut the hat from red fabric using pattern 5c, placing the edge of the pattern indicated against a fold in the fabric. Overlap the centre back edges slightly and glue. Stick a 1.3 cm ($\frac{1}{2}$ in.) wide strip of white fleecy fabric round the lower edge of the hat. Make a small bobble from white fleecy fabric and sew it to the pointed end of the hat. Place the hat on the head having the join at the centre back. Glue small pieces of white long pile fur fabric beneath the hat at each side of the beard for the hair, then glue the hat in position.

Cut two arms from pink felt using pattern 5d. Spread glue all round the edges, except for the top edges, then fold each arm on the fold line sticking the edges together. When the glue is dry stuff the arms with a little cotton wool.

For each sleeve cut a 4 cm by 7.5 cm ($1\frac{1}{2}$ in. by 3 in.) strip of red fabric. Wrap a sleeve around each arm overlapping and gluing the 4 cm ($1\frac{1}{2}$ in.) edges underneath the arms. Stick 1.3 cm ($\frac{1}{2}$ in.) wide strips of white fleecy fabric round the lower edge of each sleeve. Glue all the top edges of the felt arms and sleeves together then glue the top of each arm in position on the figure, as shown in the illustration, about 13 cm (5 in.) up from the base of the bottle. Secure the arms to the gown with pins until the glue is dry.

For each foot cut two pieces from black felt using pattern 5e. Glue the pieces together round the curved edges then when the glue is dry put a little cotton wool stuffing in each foot. Glue the remaining straight edges of each foot together then stick the feet underneath the bottle at the front as shown on the foot pattern.

Materials required for the sack of parcels

Small piece of hessian or other coarsely woven fabric
Twenty-five items as desired for the parcels, and scraps of paper, braid and string for wrapping them
Adhesive

To make the sack

For the sack cut a 13 cm by 28 cm (5 in. by 11 in.) strip of hessian. Turn in one 28 cm (11 in.) edge 1.3 cm ($\frac{1}{2}$ in.) for the top of the sack, and glue to neaten. Fold the strip in half right side inside and bringing the short edges together. Oversew the raw edges together then spread with glue to prevent fraying. Turn the sack right side out. Wrap the small parcels and number them 1 to 25.

Materials required for the reindeer

Fawn-coloured fleecy fabric
Wooden dowelling 46 cm (18 in.) long by 6 mm ($\frac{1}{4}$ in.) in diameter for the legs
Twigs for the antlers
Small red button for the nose
Cardboard tube about 4 cm ($1\frac{1}{2}$ in.) in diameter for the body
Black felt for the eyes
Small bells and a piece of ribbon
Cotton wool for stuffing
Adhesive

To make the reindeer

For the body cut a 9 cm ($3\frac{1}{2}$ in.) long section off the cardboard tube, then keep the remaining section for the reindeer's neck. To cover the body cut a 13 cm by 14 cm (5 in. by $5\frac{1}{2}$ in.) piece of fleecy fabric. Run a gathering thread along each 14 cm ($5\frac{1}{2}$ in.) edge with the wrong side of the fabric outside, pull up the gathers and fasten off, oversewing to neaten the raw edges. Turn right side out and place this piece of fabric over the cardboard tube body having the gathered edges at each end of the tube. Glue the remaining straight raw edges of the fleece together and to the tube and note that this join will be positioned underneath the reindeer's body.

For the neck cut a section off the remainder of the cardboard tube to make a smaller tube about 2 cm ($\frac{3}{4}$ in.) long by 2 cm ($\frac{3}{4}$ in.) in diameter. Cover the neck by gluing on a strip of fleecy fabric, then glue the neck to one end of the body as shown in the illustration (fig. 5).

Cut the head from fleecy fabric using pattern 5f. Oversew the straight edges of the head together then turn right side out. Stuff the head firmly. Run a gathering thread round close to the remaining raw edge, pull up the gathers turning in the raw edges, then fasten off. Glue two small pieces of fleecy fabric together, having the right side outside, then cut two ears from this piece using pattern 5g. Glue the lower edges of the ears to the head as illustrated. Cut two suitable bits of branched twigs for the antlers and glue them into the head in front of the ears piercing a hole for each one in the fabric with the point of the scissors. Cut two ovals of black felt for the eyes, the same size as for Santa Claus, and glue to the reindeer's head. Sew the small red button in position for the nose. Glue the head in position on top of the neck.

For the legs cut the wooden dowelling into four equal lengths. Sharpen each one to a point at one

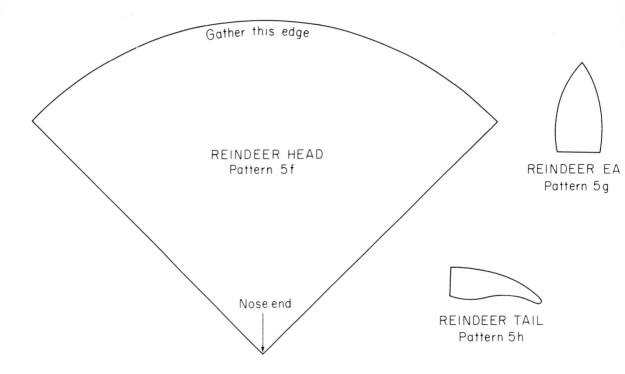

Gather this edge

REINDEER HEAD
Pattern 5f

Nose end

REINDEER EA
Pattern 5g

REINDEER TAIL
Pattern 5h

end. Pierce four holes underneath the reindeer's body with the point of the scissors, having two legs at each end. Spread glue on the pointed ends of the legs and push them through the holes into the body as far as they will go.

Cut the tail from fleecy fabric using pattern 5h, then glue it in place. Thread the bells onto a length of ribbon and tie them around the reindeer's neck.

30

Surprise clown,
a stick puppet

Figure 6 Surprise clown (happy face)

Figure 7 Surprise clown (sad face)

Here is a puppet with a dual personality (figs. 6 and 7). With one face at the back of the head and another at the front, he can be transformed from happy mood to sad in an instant, by simply turning him around. The puppet measures 40 cm (16 in.) in height and is made from an ordinary household wooden spoon. The bowl of the spoon fits inside the clown's head and the handle is covered by the clown's tunic. Seams of 1 cm ($\frac{3}{8}$ in.) are allowed on all pieces unless otherwise stated.

Materials required

One wooden spoon about 30 cm (12 in.) in length
Cuttings off nylon tights or stockings
Kapok, cotton wool or man-made fibre stuffing
Small amount of thick knitting wool
Fabric, 30 cm (12 in.) × 91 cm (36 in.)
Scraps of felt, fabric and trimmings
Red and black thread, scraps of felt and lipstick for the facial features
Adhesive

To make

For the head cut three 14 cm (5$\frac{1}{2}$ in.) long sections off a leg of the nylon stockings or tights. Put these sections inside each other to form a triple-thickness tube. Run a gathering thread round 1 cm ($\frac{3}{8}$ in.) from one lot of raw edges through all thicknesses. Pull up the gathering thread and fasten off, over-sewing securely.

Turn the head right side out and put a little stuffing in the top, then put the bowl of the spoon inside. Stuff the head all round the spoon until the head measures about 25 cm (10 in.) around. Pull the remaining raw edges of the nylon fabric down and tie a strong thread around them where the spoon bowl joins the handle.

Using patterns 6a, b and c, cut two noses from red felt, then four eyes and four eyebrows from black felt. Cut two eyelids from pink felt, as shown by the dotted line on the eye pattern.

Now using the illustrations as a guide, position the felt pieces on the head for the smiling face. Mark on the smiling mouth and the positions of the eyes. Work the mouth in red thread then make a black cross stitch at the position of each eye. Stick all the felt pieces in place. Make the sad face on the other side of the head in the same way. Colour the cheeks by rubbing in a little lipstick with a fingertip.

For the loops of hair at each side of the head, wind the strand of wool ten times around four fingers, then sew the tops of the loops to the head at one side about 1 cm ($\frac{3}{8}$ in.) above the level of the eyebrows. Sew the wool strands to the head again about 3 cm (1$\frac{1}{4}$ in.) further down. Make the hair loops at the other side of the head in the same way.

Cut the hat from felt using pattern 6d, placing the edge of the pattern indicated against a fold in the felt. Join the centre back edges then trim the seam. Turn the hat right side out and put a little stuffing in the top to shape it. Place the hat on the clown's head to cover the top of the wool loops then sew the lower edge of the hat to the head all round. Glue trimming round the lower edge of the hat and a guipure flower or ribbon rosette to the front and back as shown in the illustrations.

For the tunic cut two 25 cm by 30 cm (10 in. by 12 in.) pieces of fabric. Join the 30 cm (12 in.) edges and turn right side out, then hem one of the remaining raw edges. Turn in the other raw edge and run around a gathering thread. Place the tunic on the clown and pull up these gathers round the neck. Fasten off the thread then sew the gathers to the nylon fabric all round.

For one hand cut a 7 cm (2$\frac{3}{4}$ in.) section off the leg of the nylon tights or stockings. Fold the section in half bringing the 7 cm (2$\frac{3}{4}$ in.) edges together. Join these edges and across one end, rounding off the corners. Trim the seams and the corners then turn the hand right side out and stuff. Gather up the remaining raw edge of the hand and fasten off. Make the other hand in the same way.

For one sleeve cut a 16 cm by 18 cm (6$\frac{1}{4}$ in. by 7 in.) strip of fabric. Join the 16 cm (6$\frac{1}{4}$ in.) edges and turn right side out. Turn in one remaining raw edge 3 cm (1$\frac{1}{4}$ in.) for the wrist edge and press. Run a gathering thread around 2 cm ($\frac{3}{4}$ in.) from the wrist edge then slip the gathered end of one hand inside. Pull up the gathers and fasten off, then sew the sleeve to the hand through the gathers. Put a little stuffing in the sleeve then turn in the remaining raw edge and oversew, pulling the stitches tightly to gather. Sew this gathered edge securely to one side of the tunic close to the neck. Make the other sleeve in the same way.

Make two bows from scraps of fabric and sew to the neck of the tunic below each face.

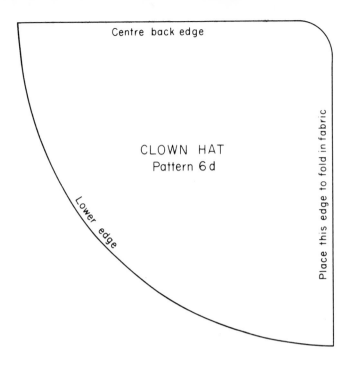

Centre back edge

CLOWN HAT
Pattern 6 d

Lower edge

Place this edge to fold in fabric

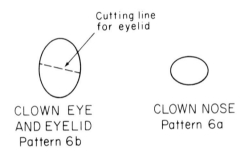

Cutting line
for eyelid

CLOWN EYE
AND EYELID
Pattern 6b

CLOWN NOSE
Pattern 6a

CLOWN EYEBROW
Pattern 6c

Pixies and toadstools

Figure 8 Pixies and toadstools

The little pixies are about 13 cm (5 in.) in height (fig. 8). They are made from pipe cleaners with beads for their heads and they can be bent into any pose. Scraps of chamois leather and suede are used for their clothes but felt could be used instead. The largest toadstool house is about 9 cm (3½ in.) in height and all the toadstools are easy to make from circles of fabric gathered up, stuffed and glued on top of cardboard tubes.

Materials required for each pixie

Two pipe cleaners
A bead or ball for the head about 1.6 cm (⅝ in.) diameter
Scraps of pink knitted-type fabric such as brushed nylon or nylon jersey
Scraps of chamois leather and suede or felt
Scraps of net fabric for the wings
Red and black ball point pens for marking on the faces
Adhesive

To make the pixie

Place the bead in the centre of a 6.5 cm (2½ in.) square of pink fabric. Gather up the fabric around the bead and tie tightly with sewing thread close to the bead. Trim off the excess fabric close to the tied thread. Mark on the facial features using the illustration as a guide, making the eyes black and the other features red.

For the legs cut one of the pipe cleaners to 13 cm (5 in.) in length. Cut a 2 cm by 14 cm (¾ in. by 5½ in.) strip of chamois leather and spread with glue. Place the pipe cleaner on the glued chamois and roll it up inside the strip to cover it. Trim each end of the chamois to a pointed shape for the pointed toes of the pixie's feet. Fold the legs strip in half and sew the folded end securely to the fabric at the base of the pixie's head.

For the arms cut one pipe cleaner to 10 cm (4 in.) in length. Bend round 6 mm (¼ in.) at each end, for the hands. Cover the hands by tying each one in the centre of a 2.5 cm (1 in.) square of pink fabric in the same way as for the head. Cover the arms in the same way as for the legs using a 2 cm by 7 cm (¾ in. by 2¾ in.) strip of chamois, leaving the hands protruding beyond the chamois strip at each end. Sew the centre of the arms piece to the back of the legs piece just below the pixie's neck.

Cut the pixie's tunic from suede or felt using pattern 7a. Snip the edges with scissors to make a fringe as shown on the pattern. Cut out the small centre hole, then cut a slit down from the hole as shown on the pattern. Put the tunic on the pixie and glue the slit edges together at the centre back. Glue the side edges together underneath the pixie's arms.

Cut the collar piece from suede or felt using pattern 7b. Snip along one edge with scissors, as shown on the pattern. Stick the collar around the pixie's neck.

Cut the hat from chamois and snip the lower edge as shown on pattern 7c. Overlap the back edges slightly and glue. Place the hat on the pixie's head, stretching it to fit, then glue it in place.

Cut the wings piece from net fabric using pattern 7d. Gather at the centre, then glue the gathered part to the back of the pixie's tunic at the top.

For the 'little tailor' pixie, glue a scrap of fabric to the left hand and sew a thread from this fabric across to the pixie's right hand, take the thread through the right hand and back again leaving a small loop of thread for the 'needle'. Stiffen the needle by spreading with glue.

Materials required for the toadstool houses

Cardboard tubes
Scraps of velvet, felt, trimmings and lace
Kapok, cotton wool or man-made fibre stuffing
Plasticine or small stones for weighting the stalks of the toadstools
Strong card
Tiny beads for the door-knobs
Adhesive

To make the largest toadstool

For the top cut an 18 cm (7 in.) diameter circle of velvet. Using very strong thread, run a gathering thread round and close to the edge of the circle. Pull up the gathers slightly and stuff the circle then pull up the gathering thread as tightly as possible leaving a 2.5 cm (1 in.) diameter opening. Fasten off the thread. Continue stuffing through the opening until the toadstool top is very firm.

For the toadstool stalk cut a 4 cm (1½ in.) section off a cardboard tube. Glue one end of the section onto a piece of strong card, then when the glue is dry, cut out the card even with the tube to form the base of the stalk. Cover the base by gluing on a circle of felt, then glue a strip of felt round the stalk to cover it.

To make the window cut a 1.6 cm by 2 cm (⅝ in. by ¾ in.) piece of black felt and onto this glue a piece of coarse net lace to form the window panes.

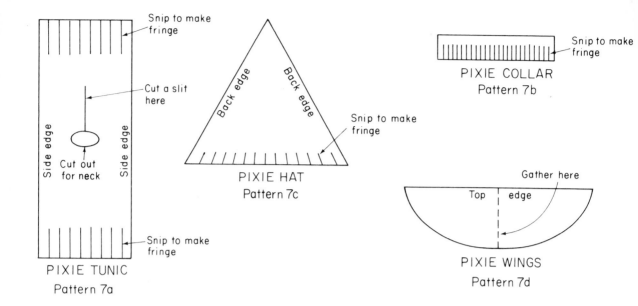

PIXIE TUNIC
Pattern 7a

Snip to make fringe

Cut a slit here

Side edge

Cut out for neck

Side edge

Snip to make fringe

PIXIE HAT
Pattern 7c

Back edge

Back edge

Snip to make fringe

PIXIE COLLAR
Pattern 7b

Snip to make fringe

PIXIE WINGS
Pattern 7d

Gather here

Top   edge

Cut the window frame from felt slightly larger than the window, round off the corners, and cut out the centre as illustrated. Glue all the window pieces in position on the stalk as illustrated. Make another window and glue it to the other side of the stalk.

For the door cut a 2 cm by 2.5 cm ($\frac{3}{4}$ in. by 1 in.) strip of fabric and glue it to the stalk beside the window. Cut a slightly larger piece of felt for the door frame, round off the top corners, and cut out the centre, then glue it in place. Glue a tiny bead to the door for a door-knob. Cut a narrow strip of felt for the door step, and a narrow strip of green felt to go round the remainder of the base of the stalk for 'grass'; glue them all in place.

Put a lump of Plasticine or a stone inside the stalk against the base then put in a little stuffing. Spread glue liberally on the top edge of the stalk, allow it to become tacky then place the toadstool on top of it. Stick pins through the gathers in the velvet and into the stalk to hold the pieces together until the glue dries.

Make another window and glue it to the top of the toadstool. Cut small circles of felt for the spots on the toadstool. Stick them to the top, then sew across each one with large stitches as shown in the illustration.

To make the medium and small toadstools
Make these in the same way as the large toadstool using the following measurements. For the medium toadstool use a 15 cm (6 in.) diameter circle for the top. Cut a section off the cardboard to make a smaller tube measuring 4 cm ($1\frac{1}{2}$ in.) diameter by 2.5 cm (1 in.) deep. Cut the door and window pieces a little smaller.

For the small toadstool use a 13 cm (5 in.) diameter circle for the top and make the stalk 3 cm ($1\frac{1}{4}$ in.) diameter by 2 cm ($\frac{3}{4}$ in.) deep. Cut the door and window pieces a little smaller than for the medium toadstool.

36

Two roly poly toys, Gnome and Pirate

Figure 9 Two roly poly toys: gnome and pirate

Here is an easy-to-make version of the traditional toy 'that won't lie down' (fig. 9). The pirate is about 13 cm (5 in.) in height and the gnome is a little taller because of his pointed hat. The centre of the rounded base of each toy is weighted, and when knocked over the toys wobble backwards and forwards until they regain their upright position. Half of a plastic play ball, about 9 cm (3½ in.) in diameter, is used for the base. However, the instructions could be adapted to suit almost any size of ball because the upper half of the toy is simply a straight strip of fabric sewn on then gathered in at the top edge. Seams and turnings on all pieces are as given in the instructions.

Materials required for both toys

A hollow plastic play ball measuring about 9 cm (3½ in.) in diameter
Plasticine, for weighting the bases
Small pieces of fabrics, felt and ric-rac braid
Kapok, cotton wool or man-made fibre stuffing
Lipstick for colouring the cheeks
A small bell for the gnome's hat
Adhesive

To make the pirate

Cut the ball in half using sharp scissors (note that there is usually a moulded seam line on plastic balls, cut along this to get two exact halves). Use only one half of the ball for the rounded base of the pirate.

To cover the base cut a 20 cm (8 in.) diameter circle of fabric. Run a gathering thread round about 2 cm (¾ in.) from the edge of the circle. Place the half ball in the centre of the circle and pull up the gathers. Turn the gathered edge of the fabric to the inside of the half ball and stick, pulling up and creasing the fabric as necessary to make it fit over the outside of the half ball as smoothly as possible.

Roll a lump of Plasticine into a sphere about the size of a golf ball. Place the Plasticine centrally inside the half ball. Pack stuffing all round the Plasticine to fill the half ball taking care not to push the Plasticine off centre.

For the body, cut a 12 cm by 32 cm (4¾ in. by 12½ in.) strip of fabric. Join the short edges of the strip taking a 1 cm (⅜ in.) seam. Turn right side out and turn in one remaining raw edge 6 mm (¼ in.). Slip this edge 1 cm (⅜ in.) over the top edge of the half ball. Now oversew this edge of the body fabric securely to the fabric covering the half ball.

Stuff the body firmly then turn in the remaining raw edge of the body fabric 1 cm (⅜ in.). Run a gathering thread round this edge, pull up the gathers very tightly, then fasten off.

For the pirate's belt cut a 2 cm (¾ in.) wide strip of felt long enough to go round the toy plus a little extra for an overlap. Stick the belt around the pirate to cover the join in the base and body fabrics.

Using pattern 8a cut the buckle shape from felt and stick it in place on the belt as shown in the illustration.

Cut the face piece from pink felt using pattern 8b. Sew this piece in position on the body, having the top of the face even with the gathers at the top of the toy as indicated on the pattern. For the beard cut a strip of felt using pattern 8c. Snip the lower portion of the beard to make a fringe as indicated on the pattern. Stretch the beard strip along the snipped edge to make a curved shape. Sew the unsnipped edge of the beard to the face at the position shown on the face pattern, easing it to fit the curve.

Cut the facial features to the sizes shown on the face pattern, the eyes from black felt, the nose from red felt and the eyebrows to match the beard. Glue them in place, then colour the cheeks with lipstick.

For the pirate's headscarf cut a 10 cm by 32 cm (4 in. by 12½ in.) strip of fabric then fray out all the raw edges a little. Place the strip around the top of toy turning in one long raw edge and lapping it over the top part of the face as shown in the illustration. Gather and sew the short ends of the scarf to one side of the head. Fold in and pleat the remaining raw edge on top of the head so that the head is completely covered, then catch the folds in place with a few stitches. Sew the lower edge of the scarf to the head all round.

To make the gnome

Make in the same way as for the pirate except for the hat. Position the eyebrows on top of the eyes as shown in the illustration.

Cut the hat from fabric using pattern 8d, placing the edge of the pattern indicated against a fold in the fabric. Join the centre back edges taking a 6 mm (¼ in.) seam. Turn the hat right side out and put a little stuffing in it. Turn in the remaining raw edge 6 mm (¼ in.), and put the hat on the head, lapping it over the top of the face at the centre front, and having the centre back seam of the hat just above the gnome's belt. Sew the hat to the head all round the lower edge then stick on a strip of ric-rac braid. Sew the bell to the point of the hat, then bend the point of the hat over to one side and catch it in this position with a few stitches.

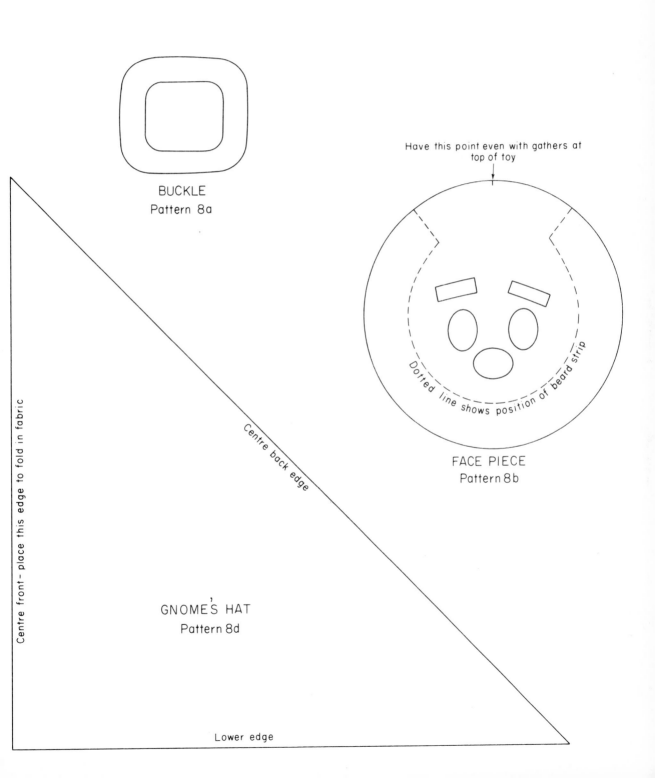

BEARD STRIP
Pattern 8c

Snip this portion all along up to this dotted line

BUCKLE
Pattern 8a

Have this point even with gathers at top of toy

Dotted line shows position of beard strip

FACE PIECE
Pattern 8b

Centre front – place this edge to fold in fabric

Centre back edge

GNOME'S HAT
Pattern 8d

Lower edge

Six dolls in historical costume

Figure 10 Six dolls in historical costume of the 14th, 15th, 16th, 17th, 18th and 19th centuries

For the costume doll enthusiast here is a collection of six dolls portraying costumes from the 14th to the 19th century (see fig. 10 and colour plate 2). The dolls, made from ordinary wooden clothes pegs, are about 12 cm (4¾ in.) in height. A pipe cleaner is used for the arms, the ends being bent around to form the hands, then covered with nylon stocking or tights fabric. All the items of clothing are glued directly onto the pegs. The types of fabric and colours most suitable for each costume are given in the instructions for each doll. Sewing thread or knitting wool is used for the dolls' hair. The gold string and braids mentioned in the instructions are the kind used for gift wrapping. Brown velvet ribbon is excellent for making fur trimmings on the tiny costumes as it really does look like fur pile in minia-ture. The narrowest available ribbons, lace edging

and braids should be used for trimming the costumes and these can be cut even narrower if they are first spread with glue on the wrong side and then allowed to dry, to prevent fraying. Seams, turnings and overlaps on all the garments are 3 mm (⅛ in.) unless otherwise stated. All the bodice pieces should be overlapped and glued at the centre back of each doll (fig. 11).

Materials required for the basic peg doll

A wooden clothes peg
Sandpaper
Cuttings off nylon tights or stockings
A pipe cleaner
A small lump of Plasticine about the size of a golf ball
Adhesive

Figure 11 Back view of six dolls in historical costume

To make the basic peg doll

Sandpaper the top of the peg to make it smooth and round for the doll's head. The face should be drawn on with pencil after the doll has been clothed using the illustration as a guide. Note that the 17th and 18th century dolls have beauty spots. Mark on the face as though the head is turned to one side for a realistic effect and put a touch of red pencil on the mouth and cheeks.

For the arms cut the pipe cleaner to 15 cm (6 in.) in length. Fold round 1.3 cm ($\frac{1}{2}$ in.) at each end of the pipe cleaner for the hands. To cover one hand cut a 2.5 cm (1 in.) diameter circle from double thickness nylon stocking or tights fabric. Put the hand in the centre of the circle and pull the raw edges of the circle tightly back along the pipe cleaner. Tie a strand of sewing thread tightly around at the position of the wrist, then cut off the excess nylon fabric, and glue the remaining raw edges of the fabric to the pipe cleaner. Cover the other hand in the same way.

The arms will next be covered with fabric for the sleeves and details are given in the instructions for each doll. After gluing the sleeves in place, stick the centre of the arms to the centre back of the doll 6 mm ($\frac{1}{4}$ in.) down from the neck. Bend the pipe cleaner arms round and down to form the shoulders then bend the arms towards the front of the doll.

To make the doll stand upright, embed the ends of the peg in a small lump of Plasticine.

To make the 14th century (c.1380) costume

Suitable fabrics are silk, satin, taffeta, and gold or silver cloth. Suitable colours are green, red and blue. (See figure 12.)

For the dress bodice and sleeves use 2.5 cm (1 in.) wide ribbon. Glue a strip of ribbon for the bodice around the peg 1.3 cm ($\frac{1}{2}$ in.) below the neck. Glue another strip around the peg below the first strip. For the belt glue a strip of gold braid around the peg where the ribbon strips join. Cut an 11.5 cm ($4\frac{1}{2}$ in.) long strip of ribbon for the sleeves, turn in the raw edges at the ends and glue to neaten. Wrap the ribbon strip around the doll's arms overlapping and gluing the long edges to make close fitting sleeves. Now glue the centre of the arms piece in position at the back of the doll.

Trace the sideless gown pattern 9a off the page onto thin paper placing a fold in the paper against the line indicated on the pattern. Cut out the paper pattern and open up to give the full sized pattern. Glue this pattern onto a piece of fabric. Cut out the fabric 3 mm ($\frac{1}{8}$ in.) larger all round than the pattern. Turn this extra 3 mm ($\frac{1}{8}$ in.) to the wrong side and stick down. For lining the top part of the gown, cut pieces of ribbon to match the dress bodice and stick to the inside of the gown as shown by the dotted lines on the pattern. Overlap and glue the centre back edges of the gown. Run a gathering thread along the front edge of the gown as shown on the pattern, pull up the gathers slightly and fasten off. Stroke and pinch the gown into small creases along the length to form folds; the paper lining will hold the creases in place. Put the gown on the doll, then stick the top back edge in place even with the top of the arms piece. Glue the front gathered edge to the front of the doll. Insert the peg ends in the lump of Plasticine. Now crease the gown again, flattening and spreading out the hem edge all round the doll as shown in the illustration.

For the decorative front piece on the sideless gown use a 4.5 cm ($1\frac{3}{4}$ in.) long strip of 1.3 cm ($\frac{1}{2}$ in.) wide braid. Turn in one end and stick, to neaten. Turn in the other end and glue to make a V-point. Stick the front piece to the centre front of the doll lapping the V-point over the gathered front edge of the gown.

For the white fur trimming round the armholes of the gown use white piping cord. Glue the cord from the back of the neck down each side of the decorative front piece then round each armhole of the gown. For an 'ermine' effect, mark the piping cord at intervals with a black marker pen.

Mark on the doll's face. For the hair, wind black thread twenty times round two fingers. Tie this small hank at the centre with a strand of thread. Glue the tied centre to the doll's head above the forehead then glue the looped ends toward the back of the head. Make another small hank and glue it in place to cover the remainder of the head.

For the templers — the side pieces of the head-dress — use braid about 6 mm ($\frac{1}{4}$ in.) in width. Cut two 2.5 cm (1 in.) strips of the braid, spread with glue, roll each one up tightly round a needle then slide it off the needle. Glue one to each side of the face as shown in the illustration. Stick a length of gold string across the forehead above the side pieces. For the veil cut a 6.5 cm ($2\frac{1}{2}$ in.) diameter circle of single thickness paper tissue. Fold the veil in half and glue the folded edge to the top of the head and down each side behind the templers. Gently crease the veil into folds at the back of the head.

Right   **Figure 12** 14th-century costume doll

To make the 15th century (c.1460) costume

Suitable fabrics are gold and silver cloth, velvet, silk, satin and taffeta. Suitable colours are red, black, green and blue. (See figure 13.)

Trace the dress skirt pattern 9b off the page onto thin paper placing a fold in the paper against the line indicated on the pattern. Cut out the paper pattern and open up to give the full sized pattern. Stick the pattern onto a piece of fabric. Cut out the fabric 3 mm ($\frac{1}{8}$ in.) larger all round than the pattern except for the waist edge, cut this even with the pattern. Turn the extra 3 mm ($\frac{1}{8}$ in.) to the wrong side and stick down. Overlap and glue the centre back edges of the skirt. Run a gathering thread round the waist edge and crease the skirt into pleats and folds down the length; the paper lining will hold the creases in place. Put the skirt on the doll and stick the waist edge in position 2 cm ($\frac{3}{4}$ in.) down from the neck, pulling up the gathers to fit. Insert the peg ends in the lump of Plasticine. Continue creasing the skirt into folds, then flatten and spread out the hem edge on the ground as shown in the illustration.

For the sleeves cut a 2.5 cm by 10 cm (1 in. by 4 in.) strip of fabric. Turn in the 2.5 cm (1 in.) edges and stick down to neaten. Wrap the strip around the arms piece overlapping and gluing the long edges to make close fitting sleeves. For the fur cuffs, stick narrow strips of brown velvet around the wrist edge of each sleeve. Glue the centre of the arms piece in position at the back of the doll.

For the undergown bodice glue a small square of ribbon to the front of the doll 6 mm ($\frac{1}{4}$ in.) below the neck. Lift the dress skirt at one side and stick to one of the doll's hands, creasing the skirt into natural folds as shown in the illustration. Now glue a strip of ribbon to match the undergown bodice to this lifted side of the dress on the inside of the skirt as shown in the illustration.

For the dress collar glue a strip of brown velvet ribbon to match the cuffs around the back of the neck and down each side of the undergown bodice.

For the belt, glue a strip of narrow braid around the top raw edge of the dress skirt to cover all the raw edges.

Mark on the doll's face and stick a bit of gold string around the neck for a necklace.

Cut the head-dress pattern 9c from paper then stick this paper pattern on to a piece of fabric and cut out the fabric even with the paper pattern. Put the head-dress on the doll's head and overlap the back edges as necessary to make the head-dress fit. Stick the back edges as overlapped, then glue the head-dress on the doll's head at the angle shown in the illustration.

For the veil use very fine net fabric. Make the veil pattern by drawing out a 35.5 cm (14 in.) diameter semi-circle with a 10 cm (4 in.) diameter semi-circle cut out of the centre. Cut the veil from fabric then glue the inner curved edge around the lower edge of the head-dress. Arrange the veil in folds down the back of the doll and stick the lower edges to the hem of the skirt if necessary to make it hang straight down.

For the face edging piece of the head-dress, cut a 4 cm ($1\frac{1}{2}$ in.) length of 1.3 cm ($\frac{1}{2}$ in.) wide bias binding. Spread it with glue on the wrong side and fold along the length. Glue the strip around the face as shown on the illustration, stretching the binding to curve it into shape.

To make the 16th century (c.1530) costume

Suitable fabrics are taffeta, velvet, silk, and satin. Note that the undergown on this doll is made from cuttings off an old neck tie (see fig. 14). Men's ties often have very tiny woven designs which are exactly right for dressing small scale dolls. Suitable colours are red, black, blue, green and orange.

For the dress bodice, glue a 2.5 cm (1 in.) wide strip of fabric round the peg 1.3 cm ($\frac{1}{2}$ in.) below the neck.

For the dress sleeves cut a 2 cm by 7.5 cm ($\frac{3}{4}$ in. by 3 in.) strip of fabric. Wrap the strip around the arms piece overlapping and gluing the long edges. For the lace ruffles at the wrists, glue on narrow strips of lace edging.

For each undergown sleeve cut a 2.5 cm by 5 cm (1 in. by 2 in.) strip of fabric, turn in the 5 cm (2 in.) edges and run a gathering thread along each one pulling up the gathers to fit around the doll's arms and wrists. Glue the undersleeves in place overlaping and sticking the 2.5 cm (1 in.) edges. Glue the centre of the arms piece in position at the back of the doll.

For the neck edging on the dress bodice stick on a strip of very narrow lace then a bit of gold string as shown in the illustration. For the gold brooch at the front of the bodice, tie a few knots in a bit of gold string then glue the knotted piece in place.

Cut the dress skirt from fabric using pattern 9d. Turn in the lower and front edges and glue to neaten. For the undergown piece which is visible at the

Left **Figure 13** 15th-century costume doll

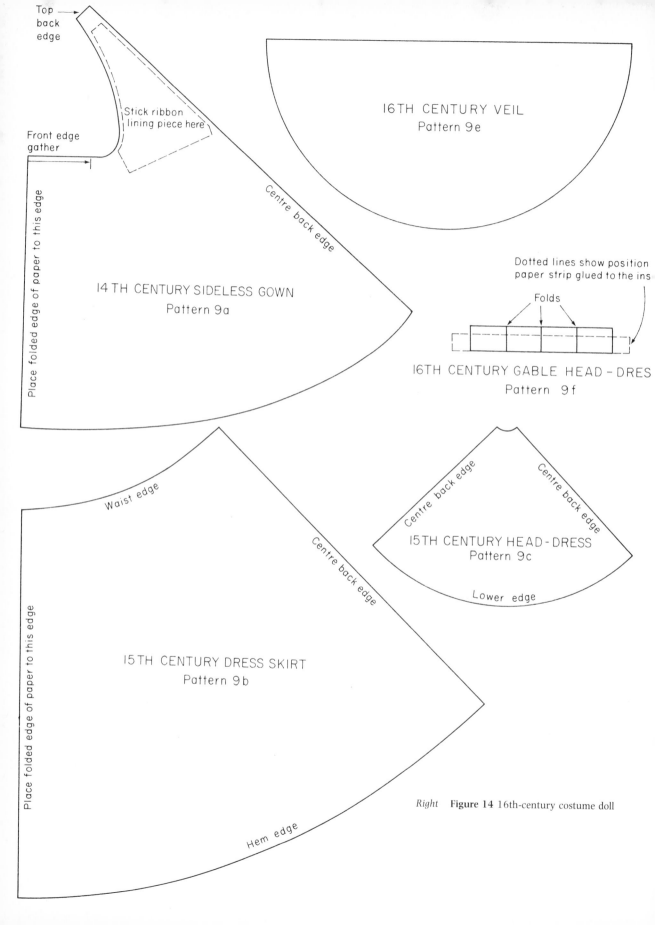

Top back edge

Stick ribbon lining piece here

Front edge gather

Place folded edge of paper to this edge

Centre back edge

14 TH CENTURY SIDELESS GOWN
Pattern 9a

16TH CENTURY VEIL
Pattern 9e

Dotted lines show position paper strip glued to the ins

Folds

16TH CENTURY GABLE HEAD–DRES
Pattern 9f

Waist edge

Centre back edge

Place folded edge of paper to this edge

15TH CENTURY DRESS SKIRT
Pattern 9b

Hem edge

Centre back edge

Centre back edge

15TH CENTURY HEAD-DRESS
Pattern 9c

Lower edge

Right **Figure 14** 16th-century costume doll

front of the costume, cut a 4 cm by 9 cm (1½ in. by 3½ in.) strip of fabric. Turn in one short edge and glue to neaten for the lower edge. Now take the dress skirt and lap the front edges over the long edges of the undergown piece, tapering from the hem to the top edge to form a triangle. Glue the front skirt edges in position on the undergown piece. Turn in the waist edge of the skirt 6 mm (¼ in.) and run round a gathering thread then put the skirt on the doll. Insert the peg ends in the lump of Plasticine then adjust the waist height of the skirt so that the hem edge touches the ground. Pull up the waist gathers tightly and fasten off.

For the girdle tie a length of gold string around the waist, knot it at the centre front then twist the ends of the string together. Thread on a small bead and knot and cut off the string to the length shown in the illustration.

For each fur sleeve, cut a 10 cm (4 in.) long strip of 2 cm (¾ in.) wide brown velvet ribbon. Overlap and glue the short edges of each strip. Turn the sleeves inside out then turn back one of the edges 3 mm (⅛ in.) and glue. Turn the sleeves right side out. Put one sleeve on each arm having the folded edges toward the front of the doll. Stick the back edges of each sleeve together all the way up to the arms. Put a dab of glue inside each sleeve where it touches the arm to hold it in position.

Mark on the doll's face, then for the hair cut a 2 cm (¾ in.) length of gold braid or cord. Spread the ends of the piece with glue to prevent fraying then glue to the head above the forehead. Alternatively a length of pipe cleaner can be used covering it with gold thread wound round and round.

Cut the veil from black fabric using pattern 9e. Glue the centre of the straight edge to the head just behind the hair then glue it down each side of the head. Arrange the veil in folds at the back keeping them in place with a dab of glue.

Cut the gable head-dress strip from paper using pattern 9f. Fold the paper strip at the solid lines indicated on the pattern thus forming the gable shape. On the outside of the gable shape glue a strip of trimming or fabric to cover it. On the inside glue a strip of white paper cut to size shown by the dotted lines on the head-dress pattern. Glue the gable head-dress in position on the doll's head then curl up the ends of the white paper strip as illustrated.

To make the 17th century (c.1625) costume

Suitable fabrics are satin, silk and taffeta. Suitable colours are yellow, blue, red, white and green. (See figure 15).

For the underskirt cut a 9 cm by 14 cm (3½ in. by 5½ in.) strip of fabric. Turn in one 14 cm (5½ in.) edge and glue for the hem of the skirt. Overlap and glue the 9 cm (3½ in.) edges. Run a gathering thread round the remaining raw edge and put the skirt on the doll having the overlap at the back of the doll. Insert the peg ends in the lump of Plasticine then pull up the skirt gathers and stick the waist edge of the skirt in place so that the hem edge touches the ground.

Cut the stomacher pattern 9g from paper, stick it onto a piece of fabric then cut out the fabric even with the paper pattern. Stick the stomacher in place at the front of the doll having the top edge 1.3 cm (½ in.) below the neck and lapping the lower edges over the gathered edge of the underskirt.

For the overskirt cut a 10 cm by 14 cm (4 in. by 5½ in.) strip of fabric. Turn in all the raw edges and stick except for one 14 cm (5½ in.) edge. Turn in and run a gathering thread along the remaining raw edge. Pull up the gathers then glue this edge in place around the back waist of the doll having the straight edges at the front lapping over the side edges of the stomacher. Glue strips of braid or trimming down the sides of the stomacher and down each side of the overskirt. Stick the front edges of the overskirt to the underskirt.

For the belt glue a strip of very narrow ribbon round the top of the overskirt then stick on a tiny bow at the centre front of the belt.

To make the arms, cover the hands in the usual way, then pull the edges of the nylon fabric further back up the arm toward the elbows. Tie round at the positions of the elbows with thread and finish off as for the wrists.

For the sleeves cut a 5 cm by 9 cm (2 in. by 3½ in.) strip of fabric to match the overskirt. Overlap and glue the 9 cm (3½ in.) edges of the strip. Put the sleeve piece on the arms, run a gathering thread round each raw edge then pull up the gathers and fasten off at elbow length. Glue a bit of braid down each sleeve to match the skirt braid.

For each lace cuff, gather up a 4cm (1½ in.) length of 1.3 cm (½ in.) wide lace edging. Glue one around the lower edge of each sleeve as shown in the illustration pulling up the gathers to fit the arms.

Gather the centre of the sleeves slightly then glue the arms in position at the back of the doll.

Page 48   **Figure 15** 17th-century costume doll

Facing page 48   See-saw Margery Daw and the Teddy Bears' picnic

Opposite   Six dolls in historical costume

For the collar gather up a 9 cm (3½ in.) length of lace edging to match the cuffs and glue it around the neck as illustrated. Knot a bit of gold string and glue the knot to the collar for a brooch.

Mark on the doll's face including the beauty spots. For the hair use short lengths of knitting wool pulled apart to make very fine strands. Glue on looped lengths of wool down each side of the face, then from the forehead to the back of the head, then across the back of the head. Finally stick a small twist of wool to the crown of the head for a bun. Glue a tiny ribbon rosette to each side of the bun.

To make the 18th century (c.1760) costume
Suitable fabrics are silk and cotton prints. Suitable colours are white, or pale colours with tiny printed flowers or stripes. (See figure 16.)

For the dress bodice glue a 2.5 cm (1 in.) wide strip of fabric round the peg 1.3 cm (½ in.) below the neck.

Cut two skirt pieces from firm material such as dress interlining, using pattern 9h. Trim 6 mm (¼ in.) off the lower edge of each piece. Cut two skirt pieces from fabric using the pattern. Turn in the lower edge of each fabric piece and glue, to neaten. Sandwich the fabric pieces, right sides together, between the interlining pieces having the waist edges and side edges even. Join the side edges stitching through all thicknesses. Trim the seam. Now make a dart across the skirt at each side through all thicknesses, as shown on the pattern. Turn the skirt right side out.

Spread a little glue around the doll at the position of the waist then push the end of the peg through the waist edges of the skirt until the waist edge of the skirt is round the doll's waist. Note that the waist edges of the skirt will turn inwards as this is done. Insert the ends of the peg in the lump of Plasticine and adjust the skirt height to touch the ground, before the glue dries.

Cut the front panel of the skirt to the size shown on the skirt pattern using plain fabric. Turn in the lower edge and glue. Glue strips of lace trimming across the panel to cover it, all the way up. Glue the panel to the front of the skirt.

For the front bodice piece, cut a triangle of plain fabric 1.3 cm (½ in.) wide at the neck tapering to the waist. Glue it in position on the doll. Mark on lines for the lacing on this piece as illustrated, using a

Left **Figure 16** 18th-century costume doll

ball point pen. Glue a strip of narrow lace and a bow made from thread, to the neck edge.

Make the arms as for the 17th century doll. For each of the sleeve frills gather up a 5 cm (2 in.) strip of 1.3 cm (½ in.) wide lace edging. Glue around the arms at the elbows. For the sleeves cut a 2.5 cm by 7.5 cm (1 in. by 3 in.) strip of fabric. Turn in the short edges of the strip and glue, to neaten. Wrap the strip around the arms overlapping and gluing the long edges. Glue the elbow edges of the sleeves over the edges of the lace frills.

Decorate the sleeve edges by gluing on narrow lace trimming and bows made from thread. Glue the arms in position at the back of the doll. Glue narrow lace edging round the back of the neck and down the sides of the bodice and skirt panels. Stick a lace frill to the skirt on either side of the panel.

For the train at the back of the dress, cut a 6.5 cm by 13 cm (2½ in. by 5 in.) strip of fabric. Turn in and glue all the raw edges then stick on lace trimming except for one 6.5 cm (2½ in.) edge. Gather this edge tightly and glue it to the back neck edge of the dress bodice.

Mark the face on the doll including the beauty spot then tie a length of black sewing thread round the neck for a ribbon necklace. The hair is made by winding white sewing thread round short lengths of pipe cleaner to cover them completely. These are then bent to shape and glued to the head. For the first curl above the face, place two 2.5 cm (1 in.) lengths of pipe cleaner together, cover with thread, holding the ends of the thread in place with dabs of glue. For the next curl use a 5 cm (2 in.) length of pipe cleaner and glue it to the head behind the first curl, letting one end hang down over the doll's shoulder for a ringlet. Cover the back of the doll's head with a small hank of thread made by winding the thread a few times round two fingers. Glue the hank in place on the back of the head. Make a few more pipe cleaner curls and glue to the top of the doll's head to heighten the hair style then stick on a few tiny feathers and bits of lace.

To make the 19th century (c. 1850) costume
Suitable fabrics are silk, taffeta and cotton. Suitable colours are stripes and plaids in dark colours. Note that 1.4 m (1½ yd) of 4 cm (1½ in.) wide ribbon is required for making the dress. (See figure 17.)

For the dress bodice glue a strip of ribbon round the peg just below the neck. Glue a strip of lace edging down the centre front of the bodice and stick a tiny bead at the neck edge for a brooch.

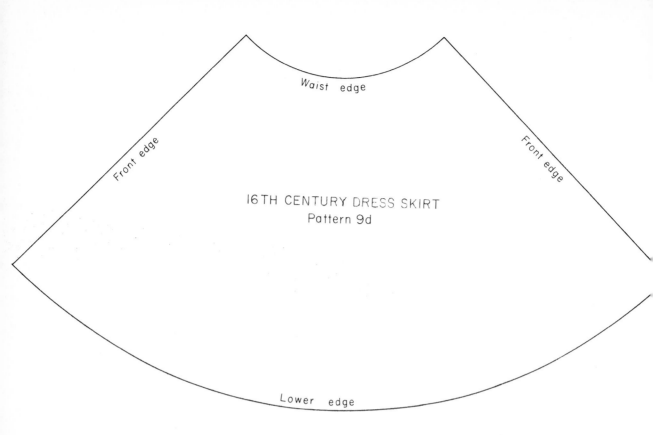

16TH CENTURY DRESS SKIRT
Pattern 9d

Waist edge

Front edge

Front edge

Lower edge

To make the foundation for the frilled skirt, cut a 9 cm by 18 cm ($3\frac{1}{2}$ in. by 7 in.) strip of fabric. Turn in one 18 cm (7 in.) edge and stick, to neaten for the hem edge. For the first frill cut a 35.5 cm (14 in.) length of ribbon and gather one long edge to measure 18 cm (7 in.). Glue this edge to the skirt having the ungathered long edge even with the hem of the skirt. Flatten the gathered ribbon into folds and pleats and stick to the skirt fabric if necessary here and there to hold in place. Cut, then gather another 35.5 cm (14 in.) length of ribbon and stick it to the skirt 2.5 cm (1 in.) above the top edge of the first frill. Overlap and glue the ends of the frills and the short edges of the skirt. Run a gathering thread round the remaining raw edge of the skirt and put it on the doll. Insert the ends of the peg in the lump of Plasticine. Pull up the skirt gathers and fasten off so that the hem of the skirt touches the ground.

For the top skirt frill cut a 25.5 cm (10 in.) length of ribbon then overlap and glue the short edges.

Gather up one long edge, put the frill on the doll and pull up and fasten off the gathers round the waist. Crease the frill and stick in place as for the other frills.

For each lace undersleeve, cut a 5 cm (2 in.) long strip of 2 cm ($\frac{3}{4}$ in.) wide lace edging. Lap and glue the short edges of each strip then put them on the doll's arms and gather the remaining edges to fit the wrists and arms. For the sleeves cut a 10 cm (4 in.) length of ribbon. Turn in the ends of the strip and glue, to neaten. Wrap the ribbon strip round the arms overlapping and gluing the long edges at the wrists then lapping these edges a little more at the centre of the strip to make tapered sleeves. Glue the arms in position at the back of the doll.

To make the pieces which go from the waist over each shoulder, cut a piece of ribbon 13 cm

Right   **Figure 17** 19th-century costume doll

52

(5 in.) long by 2 cm ($\frac{3}{4}$ in.) in width. Fold this in half along the length and glue, making a 1 cm ($\frac{3}{8}$ in.) wide strip. Cut this strip in two pieces then cut one end of each piece to a point so that when these edges are stuck together they form a V-point. Stick the V-point to the centre front of the doll's skirt just below the waist then stick each strip over the shoulders and lap them at the back waist edge, cutting the ends if necessary to the correct length.

Mark on the doll's face. For the hair, wind sewing thread about thirty times round two fingers. Tie this small hank at the centre with a length of thread. Stick the tied centre to the top of the doll's head and the looped ends down the sides of the face and towards the back. Repeat this, to cover the back of the head.

For the lace cap cut a 4.5 cm ($1\frac{3}{4}$ in.) strip of 2 cm ($\frac{3}{4}$ in.) wide lace edging. Turn in the ends and stick, to neaten. Gather up the cap about 6 mm ($\frac{1}{4}$ in.) from each end then glue on bows made from thread. Glue the cap to the head having the gathers at each side.

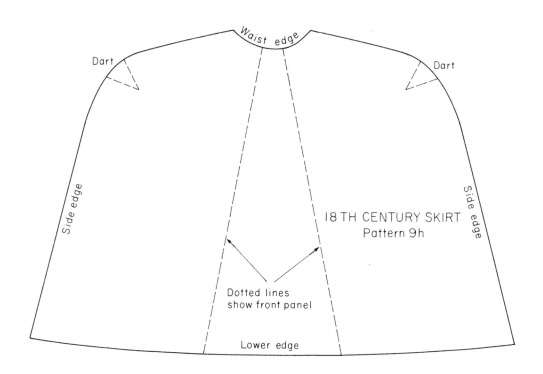

18 TH CENTURY SKIRT
Pattern 9h

Dotted lines show front panel

17TH CENTURY
STOMACHER
Pattern 9g

The teddy bears' picnic

Figure 18 Teddy bear at the teddy bears' picnic

These small cuddly bears measure about 13 cm (5 in.) in height (see fig. 18 and colour plate 3). They have lots of delicious looking things to eat for their picnic, all made from discarded household items and scraps of felt. The bears are made from fawn fleecy fabric and filled with dried lentils. Rice or pearl barley can be used instead of lentils but remember that any of these dried fillings should be removed before washing the teddies. The bears are made by the stitch-around method and the outlines on the body and head patterns are the actual stitching lines.

Materials required for the bears
Small pieces of fleecy fabric
About 56 grammes (2 oz) of lentils for each bear
Scraps of black and pink felt for the facial features
Adhesive

To make a bear
Trace the body and head patterns 10a and b off the page onto thin paper. Pin the body pattern onto two layers of fleecy fabric, having the right sides of the fabric together. Machine stitch all round close to the pattern, leaving a gap in the stitching as shown on the pattern. Remove the pattern and cut out the body about 3 mm ($\frac{1}{8}$ in.) from the stitching line. Turn right side out and fill the body with about 42 grammes ($1\frac{1}{2}$ oz) of lentils, using a small funnel shape made from paper to do this easily. Turn in the raw edges and ladder stitch the opening.

Bring the bear's arms and feet forward folding along the fold lines indicated on the pattern. Ladder stitch the arms and feet in this position as shown by the dotted lines on the pattern.

Pin the head pattern onto two layers of fabric and stitch; cut out and turn it as for the body. Work small running stitches through both thicknesses of fabric at the base of the ears as shown by the dotted lines on the pattern. Fill the head with the remainder of the lentils then turn in the raw edges and ladder stitch the opening. Place the head at the front of the body matching the points marked A on the patterns. Oversew the back of the head to the top of the body at this point only. This will allow the bear's head to be moved into different positions as shown in the illustration.

Cut the largest eye shape shown on the bear's head pattern from pink felt. Cut the smaller eye shape from black felt, then glue these eye pieces together. Glue the eyes in position on the bear's head. For the sleeping eyes cut the sleeping eyelid from pink felt using pattern 10c, then cut the small eyelash piece

from black felt. Glue the eyelash piece to the eyelid then glue the eyes in place.

Cut the nose from felt using pattern 10d. Run a gathering thread round the nose close to the edge, pull up the gathers tightly and fasten off. Sew the nose to the bear at the lower edge of the face.

Materials required for the picnic items
Scraps of fabrics and felt
Cotton wool for stuffing
A transparent plastic egg carton and a red Cellophane sweet wrapper, for the jelly
Small plastic and metal lids off grocery tins and packages, for the plates
Small brown plastic pill containers for the jars of honey, measuring about 2.5 cm (1 in.) diameter by 3 cm ($1\frac{1}{4}$ in.) deep
Two large-size matchboxes measuring about 7.9 × 4.5 × 1.4 cm ($3\frac{1}{8}$ × $1\frac{3}{4}$ × $\frac{1}{2}$ in.), such as a 'Swan Vestas' matchbox, and 1.2 m ($1\frac{1}{4}$ yd) of 1.3 cm ($\frac{1}{2}$ in.) wide brown braid, for the picnic basket
Brown and yellow pencils or felt-tipped pens
Adhesive

To make the picnic table cloth and cushion
For the cloth cut a 15 cm (6 in.) square of fabric and fray out the edges.

For the cushion cut two 7 cm ($2\frac{3}{4}$ in.) squares of fabric. Join them round the edges taking a narrow seam and leaving one side open. Turn the cushion right side out, stuff, then turn in and slip stitch the remaining raw edges.

To make the bread and butter
For each slice of bread cut a 2 cm ($\frac{3}{4}$ in.) square of white felt. Colour all round the edges with the moistened tip of a brown pencil or use a brown felt-tipped pen. Cut the slice of bread diagonally across, then colour each piece with yellow pencil or pen, for the butter.

To make the swiss roll
Cut a 4 cm by 6.5 cm ($1\frac{1}{2}$ in. by $2\frac{1}{2}$ in.) strip of yellow felt and a strip of red felt the same size. Stick the red strip on top of the yellow strip then spread the red strip with glue and roll the swiss roll up along the 6.5 cm ($2\frac{1}{2}$ in.) length. Use sharp scissors to cut off individual slices when the glue is dry.

To make the jelly
Cut one section off the transparent plastic egg carton about 2.5 cm (1 in.) deep. Push a piece of red

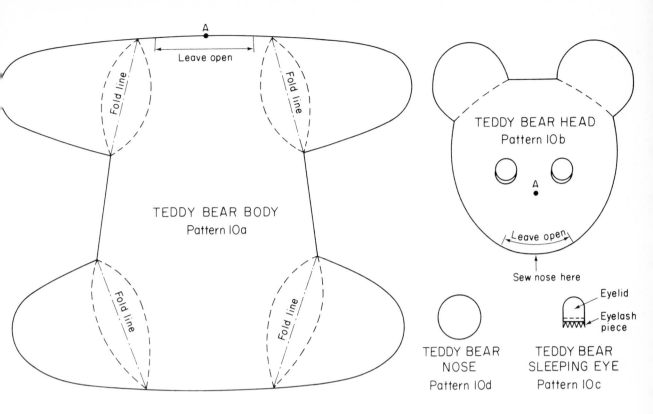

A

Leave open

Fold line

Fold line

TEDDY BEAR BODY
Pattern 10a

Fold line

Fold line

TEDDY BEAR HEAD
Pattern 10b

A

Leave open

Sew nose here

Eyelid

Eyelash
piece

TEDDY BEAR
NOSE

Pattern 10d

TEDDY BEAR
SLEEPING EYE

Pattern 10c

Cellophane inside the section, then glue the jelly onto a plastic lid.

To make the jars of honey

Note that plastic pill containers may be of a suitable diameter but too tall. These can be cut down to size if desired using a saw.

Make small labels for the honey jars and stick them in place. Tie a circle of greaseproof paper on the top.

To make the pie

Use a small metal lid for the pie dish. Cut a circle of light brown felt to fit on top of the pie dish, for the pastry. Snip small V-shaped slits in the centre of the pastry, then put a little stuffing in the pie dish. Stretch the top of the pastry slightly to fit over the stuffing, then stick it to the pie dish all round the edge. For the crimped effect round the edge of the pie, press the felt with the edge of a hot iron at intervals all round. Use a brown pencil or pen to darken the colour of the pastry here and there.

To make the picnic basket

Use the tray parts of the matchboxes only. Place one tray on top of the other to form the lid and base of the basket. Hinge them together along one long edge by sticking on a strip of adhesive tape.

Cover the top and base of the basket by sticking on strips of braid side by side, then stick braid round the sides of the top and base. Make a small loop of thread and a toggle fastening from a bit of a matchstick, then glue one to the top and one to the base at the front edge. Make a loop of thread for a handle and glue it in place. Line the basket with pieces of fabric cut to fit.

Four pop-up toys

Figure 19 Four pop-up toys: chimney sweep, pirate, princess and Santa Claus

These four characters are about 15 cm (6 in.) high. When the rod at the base of each toy is pulled and pushed, the figure pops in and out of the cardboard tube (figs. 19 and 20). The figures can also be given extra movements by twisting the rods to left and right.

Materials required

Cardboard tubes measuring about 4 cm (1½ in.) diameter

Plastic ball point pens (with the ink cartridges removed), or empty plastic felt-tipped pens, or pencils, for the rods

Scraps of fabrics, paper, card, trimmings, nylon stockings or tights, felt, cotton wool or other stuffing, fur fabric, embroidery thread

Adhesive

To make the basic toy

Cut a 6.5 cm (2½ in.) long section off a cardboard tube. Cut a circle of strong card to fit one end of the section of tube then cut a small hole in the centre of

the circle of card just large enough for the pen or pencil to be pushed through. Glue the card circle to one end of the tube. Note that two or three layers of thin card can be glued together if necessary to make this end strong enough.

To make the head, cut a 4.5 cm (1¾ in.) diameter circle of stocking or tights fabric. Run a gathering thread round, about 6 mm (¼ in.) from the edge, then stuff the centre of the circle, pulling up the gathers slightly, to make the head about 7.5 cm (3 in.) in circumference. Spread the pointed end of a pen or pencil with glue, push it into the head, then pull up the gathering thread tightly and fasten off. Work the facial features for each toy with small stitches as illustrated, using black thread for the eyes and red thread for the noses and mouths. Colour the cheeks with the moistened tip of a red pencil.

To make the body, cut a 5 cm (2 in.) wide strip of fabric long enough to go around the tube plus a little extra for an overlap on the 5 cm (2 in.) edges. Glue one long edge of the fabric strip 6 mm (¼ in.) onto the top outside edge of the cardboard tube, then

Figure 20 The four pop-up toys 'popped down'

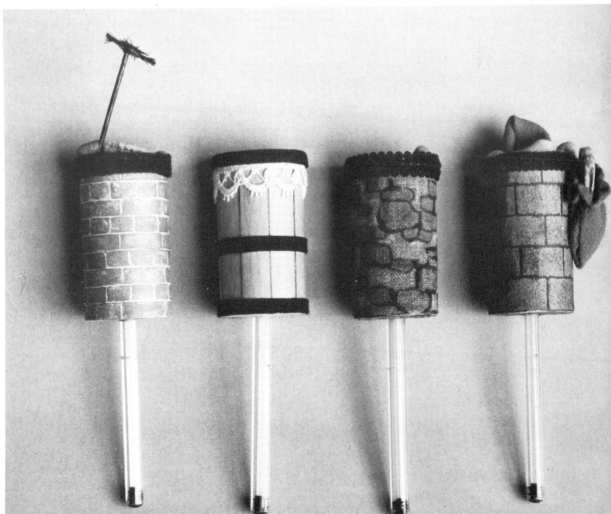

overlap and stick the 5 cm (2 in.) edges of the strip. Run a gathering thread round the remaining raw edge of the fabric strip. Push the end of the pen or pencil which is opposite the head down through the gathered edge of the fabric and through the hole in the base of the tube. Now pull up the gathering thread around the neck of the figure and fasten off then oversew the body fabric to the nylon fabric at the neck.

For each arm cut a 3 cm ($1\frac{1}{4}$ in.) square of fabric. Overlap two opposite edges of each square 3 mm ($\frac{1}{8}$ in.) and stick. For each hand cut a 2.5 cm (1 in.) diameter circle of stocking or tights fabric then run a gathering thread round the edge and put a little stuffing in the centre. Pull up the thread and fasten off, then glue the gathered end of each hand into one end of each arm. Put a little stuffing in each arm then glue the top edges of the arms to either side of the figure close to the neck.

Cover the outside of the cardboard tube with suitable paper or fabric as given in the instructions for each character, then glue braid or trimming around the top edge of the tube.

To make Santa Claus in a chimney

Make the basic toy using red fabric for the body and arms. Stick 3 mm ($\frac{1}{8}$ in.) wide strips of white felt round the wrist edges of the arms and around the neck. Cover the cardboard tube with stone effect paper or use coloured pencils to mark stones onto plain paper.

Using pattern 11a, cut the beard from white fur fabric or felt. Glue it in position on the face then cut out and glue on two narrow strips for the mustache as shown in the illustration.

Using pattern 11b, cut the hat from red fabric. Glue it around the head overlapping and sticking the centre back edges at the back of the head. Cut a 1.3 cm ($\frac{1}{2}$ in.) wide strip of white felt and glue it round the face edge of the hat. Bend over and stick the pointed end of the hat to one side of the head then sew a small bead to the point for a bobble.

Glue the ends of the hands to the top of the chimney at each side. Cut the sack from fabric using pattern 11c. Turn in each end at the dotted turning line shown on the pattern and stick down. Fold the strip of fabric in half at the fold line then join the raw edges at each side taking a tiny seam. Turn the sack right side out and put in a little stuffing. Run a gathering thread round 6 mm ($\frac{1}{4}$ in.) down from the top of the sack. Make a tiny parcel from a piece of folded paper, wrapped and tied with thread. Glue

the parcel inside the top of the sack then pull up the gathering thread tightly around it and fasten off. Glue the sack to one side of the chimney beside one of Santa's hands as shown in the illustration.

To make the chimney sweep in a chimney

Make the basic toy. Cover the cardboard tube with brick effect paper or use coloured pencils or pens to mark bricks onto plain paper.

Using pattern 11d, cut the hair from fur fabric. Stick it to the head easing it all round to fit. Trim off or stick down the fur pile if it is too long.

Cut the cap piece from thin card using pattern 11e, then stick the card to the wrong side of a piece of fabric which is a little larger all round. Turn over and glue the excess fabric onto the other side of the card. Use pattern 11f to cut out the cap peak and cover it with fabric in the same way. Glue the cap peak to the underside of the cap as shown on the pattern then glue the cap to the head.

For the scarf, cut a 2 cm by 13 cm ($\frac{3}{4}$ in. by 5 in.) strip of fabric. Fray out all the raw edges slightly then tie and stick the scarf around the chimney sweep's neck. Glue the ends of the hands to the top of the chimney at each side. Blacken the face, hands and clothes by rubbing them with the moistened tip of a black pencil.

For the chimney sweep's brush, cut a few bristles about 4 cm ($1\frac{1}{2}$ in.) long from a sweeping brush. Tie the bristles tightly together at the centre with thread, then bend and spread them out to make a circular brush. Trim the bristles all round to make the brush about 2.5 cm (1 in.) in diameter. Cut two 6 mm ($\frac{1}{4}$ in.) diameter circles of card and stick one to the centre of the brush on each side. Pierce a small hole in the centre of the card circle on one side and glue in one end of a cocktail stick for the brush handle. Colour the entire brush black using a marker pen or paint.

Pierce a small hole in the body fabric right beside one hand. Spread the end of the brush handle with glue and push it into this hole. Glue the brush handle to the hand at this point also. Note that the brush stays outside the chimney when the chimney sweep is pulled inside.

To make the pirate in the crow's nest

Make the basic toy. Cut the neck scarf from fabric using pattern 11g, then tie and stick it around the neck. Cut the beard from fur fabric or felt using pattern 11h, then stick it in position on the face.

Cut the headscarf from fabric using pattern 11j.

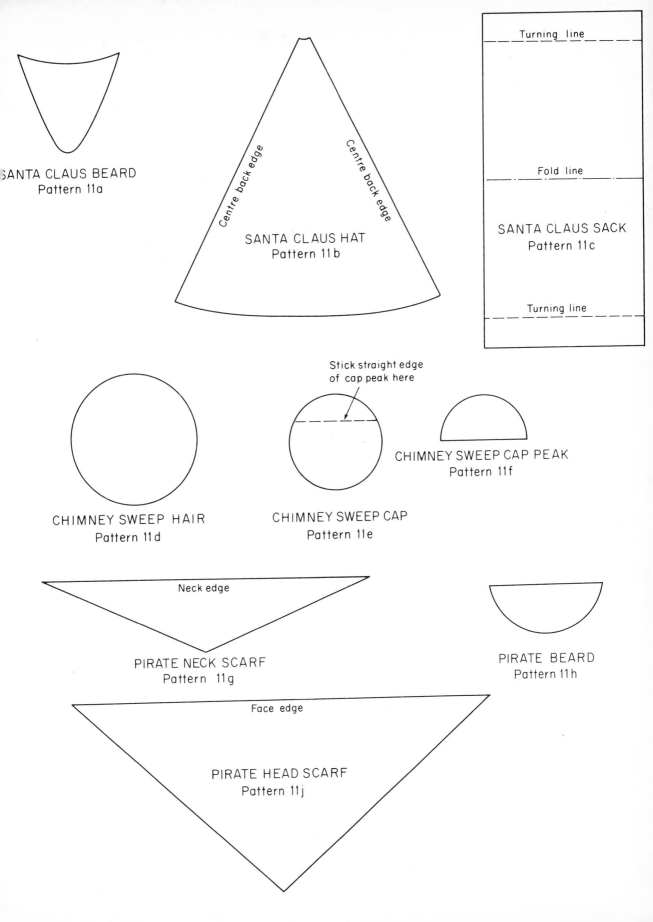

SANTA CLAUS BEARD
Pattern 11a

Centre back edge

Centre back edge

SANTA CLAUS HAT
Pattern 11b

Turning line

Fold line

SANTA CLAUS SACK
Pattern 11c

Turning line

CHIMNEY SWEEP HAIR
Pattern 11d

Stick straight edge
of cap peak here

CHIMNEY SWEEP CAP
Pattern 11e

CHIMNEY SWEEP CAP PEAK
Pattern 11f

Neck edge

PIRATE NECK SCARF
Pattern 11g

PIRATE BEARD
Pattern 11h

Face edge

PIRATE HEAD SCARF
Pattern 11j

Turn in all the raw edges a little and stick down, to neaten. Glue the scarf around the head crossing over and sticking the points at one side as shown in the illustration. Glue one hand to the forehead as illustrated.

Cover the cardboard tube with brown paper marked with pencil to resemble strips of wood. Glue a strip of lace trimming round the top edge of the tube then glue on three strips of black shoe lace as illustrated.

To make the princess in the tower

Make the basic toy. For the hair make a plait 9 cm ($3\frac{1}{2}$ in.) long from a few strands of yellow embroidery thread. Tie a thread round each end of the plait. Glue the plait around the face as shown in the illustration.

For the veil cut a bit of lace edging about 5 cm (2 in.) long. Stick it behind the plait to cover the back of the head. Glue a small circle of gold trimming to the top of the head for a crown. Stick a bit of trimming round the neck and wrist edges. Glue one hand to the face as illustrated.

Cover the cardboard tube with fabric or paper then mark on rough stones using coloured pencils, as illustrated.

To work the toys

Hold the tube in one hand and push, pull or twist the end of the pen or pencil with the other hand.

Right **Figure 21** Mary, the miniature dressing-up doll, with all her outfits

Mary, a miniature dressing-up doll

Mary measures only 16.5 cm (6½ in.) in height. She is made from pink stockinette and has six different outfits of clothes plus her very own tiny teddy bear (fig. 21). For the doll and teddy bear pattern pieces the outline is the actual stitching line and these are made by the stitch-around method. Join all other pieces taking 3 mm (⅛ in.) seams and turnings unless otherwise stated. Use thin, soft fabrics for the clothes and after sewing the seams, press, then glue the seam turnings flat to seal the raw edges and prevent fraying.

Materials required for the doll

A small piece of pink stockinette fabric
Kapok, or man-made fibre stuffing
A skein of brown embroidery thread for the hair
Black and red thread and red pencil for the facial features
Adhesive

To make the doll

Trace the body and head pattern 12a and the leg and arm patterns 12b and c off the page onto thin paper. Pin the body and head pattern onto two layers of stockinette fabric, with the 'most stretch' in the fabric going across the body as indicated on the pattern. Machine stitch the fabric round, close to the edge of the paper pattern, leaving the lower edges open as shown on the pattern. Trim off the fabric even with the lower edges of the body pattern. Remove the pattern and trim the fabric close to the stitching line all round. Turn right side out. Stuff very firmly so that the head and body measure about 9.5 cm (3¾ in.) all round at the widest parts. Catch the front of the body to the back with a few stitches at points A at the lower edges. Tie a double strand of sewing thread very tightly around the neck as shown by the dotted line on the pattern then sew the thread ends into the doll.

Using black thread work the eyes with small straight stitches 1.3 cm (½ in.) apart and half way down the face. Work three small straight stitches over each eye for the eyelashes as shown in the illustration. For the mouth, work one straight stitch using red thread, 9 mm (⅜ in.) below the eyes. Moisten the tip of the red pencil and carefully colour the cheeks, nose, and mouth below the red thread.

Sew a few small loops of embroidery thread to the head to hang down at the centre of the forehead. To make the remainder of the hair cut a 7.5 cm (3 in.) square of thick paper and wind embroidery thread around it to cover about 5 cm (2 in.). Machine

stitch through the centre of the strands and paper using matching thread, then tear the paper away. Glue the machine stitched centre of the hair to the centre parting position on the head, from the forehead towards the back of the neck. Gather the loops of embroidery thread to each side of the head and use thread to tie them in bunches. Sew the bunches to each side of the head.

To make a leg, pin the leg pattern onto two layers of stockinette fabric, with the 'most stretch' in the fabric going across the leg as indicated on the pattern. Machine stitch the fabric all round and close to the edge of the pattern, leaving the upper edges of the leg open as indicated. Trim off the fabric even with the upper edge of the leg pattern. Remove the pattern, trim the fabric close to the stitching line then turn the leg right side out. Stuff very firmly, then ladder stitch the upper edges of the leg to the lower edges of the body, matching points A, and adding more stuffing if necessary to make the join firm. Turn up the leg at the dotted line to make the foot, then ladder stitch it to the leg to hold in place as shown on the pattern. Make the knee half way down the leg by taking a stab stitch through from one side seam to the other, then through to the back of the knee. Pull the thread up tightly then fasten off. Make the other leg in the same way.

To make an arm, pin the arm pattern onto two layers of stockinette fabric, stitch, cut out, turn and stuff in the same way as for the legs. Turn in the upper raw edges of the arm and slip stitch, then sew the top of the arm to one side of the body about 6 mm (¼ in.) down from the neck. Tie thread tightly round the wrist as shown by the dotted line on the pattern, then make the elbow in the same way as the knees. Make the other arm in the same way.

Materials required for the clothes and teddy

Scraps of fabrics, thin card, felt, stuffing and trimmings
Shirring elastic
Smallest size hooks and snap fasteners
Adhesive

To make the panties

Cut out the panties placing pattern 12d to a fold as indicated. Sew narrow lace trimming to the leg edges then join one side seam. Turn in the waist edge a good 3 mm (⅛ in.) and stitch, then thread elastic through the turning to fit the waist, knotting the ends of the elastic together. Join the remaining side seam.

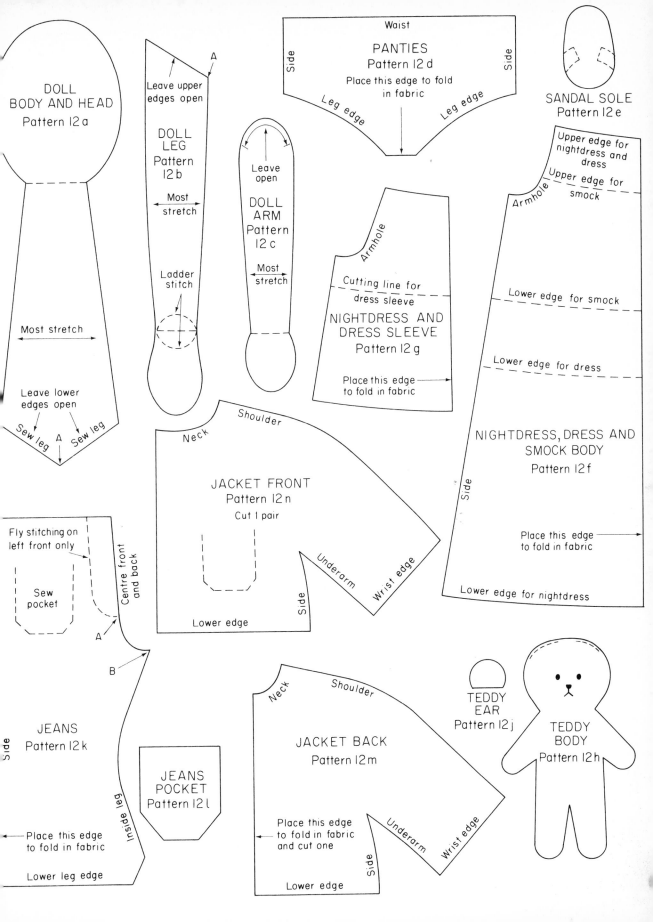

DOLL BODY AND HEAD Pattern 12 a

Most stretch

Leave lower edges open

Sew leg A Sew leg

DOLL LEG Pattern 12 b

Leave upper edges open

A

Most stretch

Ladder stitch

DOLL ARM Pattern 12 c

Leave open

Most stretch

PANTIES Pattern 12 d

Waist

Side

Side

Place this edge to fold in fabric

Leg edge

Leg edge

SANDAL SOLE Pattern 12 e

NIGHTDRESS AND DRESS SLEEVE Pattern 12 g

Armhole

Cutting line for dress sleeve

Place this edge to fold in fabric

NIGHTDRESS, DRESS AND SMOCK BODY Pattern 12 f

Upper edge for nightdress and dress

Upper edge for smock

Armhole

Lower edge for smock

Lower edge for dress

Side

Place this edge to fold in fabric

Lower edge for nightdress

JACKET FRONT Pattern 12 n Cut 1 pair

Neck

Shoulder

Side

Underarm

Wrist edge

Lower edge

JEANS Pattern 12 k

Fly stitching on left front only

Sew pocket

Centre front and back

A

B

Side

Inside leg

Place this edge to fold in fabric

Lower leg edge

JEANS POCKET Pattern 12 l

JACKET BACK Pattern 12 m

Neck

Shoulder

Side

Underarm

Wrist edge

Place this edge to fold in fabric and cut one

Lower edge

TEDDY EAR Pattern 12 j

TEDDY BODY Pattern 12 h

To make the sandals

For the straps cut two 3 mm by 4 cm ($\frac{1}{8}$ in. by 1$\frac{1}{2}$ in.) strips of felt. Using pattern 12e, cut two soles from thin card. Glue the ends of each strap to the underside of each sole as shown by the dotted lines on the sole pattern. Cut two more soles from card, and glue these under the first soles to cover the ends of the straps.

To make the nightdress

Cut out two each of the body and sleeve pieces, using the full sized patterns 12f and 12g, and placing the edges indicated on the patterns to folds in the fabric. Sew a frill of lace down the centre of one body piece as shown in the illustration (fig. 22). Join the sleeve armholes to the body armholes but leave one seam unsewn. Sew narrow lace to the neck and lower sleeve edges then sew lace to the lower edge of the nightdress about 1.3 cm ($\frac{1}{2}$ in.) up from the raw edges. Join the remaining armhole seam then the entire side and sleeve seams. Hem the lower edge of the nightdress. Thread elastic through the edge of the lace at the neck, knot the ends of the elastic making sure that it will stretch sufficiently for the nightdress to go over the doll's head. Glue the ends of the elastic down. Thread elastic through each wrist edge in the same way. Sew a small bow and beads for 'buttons' to the centre front frill.

Right   **Figure 23** Mary in jeans and jacket

To make the teddy

Pin the body pattern 12h onto a double layer of felt and machine stitch all round the felt close to the pattern, leaving a gap in the stitching at the top of the head. Remove the pattern and cut out the body close to the stitching line. Stuff the teddy, machine stitch the opening in the top of the head then sew the thread ends into the head. Cut two ears from single thickness felt using pattern 12j. Sew the lower edges of the ears in place on the head as shown on the pattern (12h). Work the facial features as shown on the pattern using black thread. Tie a bow of narrow ribbon round teddy's neck.

To make the jeans and jacket

Cut out two jeans pieces as directed on pattern 12k. Make two lines of contrasting coloured stitching down the centre of each jeans piece and continue with this colour of stitching for the whole outfit (see fig. 23). Cut two jeans pocket pieces from pattern 12l, turn in all the raw edges 3 mm ($\frac{1}{8}$ in.)

Figure 22 Mary in her nightdress with teddy bear (instructions for making the bed may be found in Goldilocks and the Three Bears section)

and glue. Sew a pocket to each jeans piece as shown by the dotted line on the pattern taking care to make a pair so that both pockets will be at the back of the jeans when they are completed. Make a line of stitching on the left front edge of one piece only, for the fly front. Join the jeans pieces at the centre back seam then at the centre front seam from point A to B. Turn in and glue the remainder of the front seam edges for the front opening. Turn in the lower leg edges 6 mm ($\frac{1}{4}$ in.) and sew in place with two rows of stitching. Turn in the waist edge and stitch in the same way. Join the inside leg edges. Sew a hook and a thread loop to the front waist edges.

For the jacket cut one back and two fronts using patterns 12m and 12n. Turn in each centre front edge 6 mm ($\frac{1}{4}$ in.) and sew in place with two rows of stitching. Cut two pockets a little smaller than for the jeans, turn in the edges and stitch to the jacket fronts in the same way as given for the jeans pockets. Join the jacket fronts to the back at the shoulder seams. Turn in the neck edge 3 mm ($\frac{1}{8}$ in.) and glue, then work two rows of stitching round it. Turn in the wrist edges 6 mm ($\frac{1}{4}$ in.) and sew in place with two rows of stitching. Join the underarm and side seams then turn up the lower edge 6 mm ($\frac{1}{4}$ in.) and sew in place with two rows of stitching. Sew hooks and thread loops to the front edges.

To make the striped sweater

Cut out one front and two backs as directed on pattern 12p. Join the centre back seam from the lower edge for 1.3 cm ($\frac{1}{2}$ in.). Turn in the remaining centre back edges 3 mm ($\frac{1}{8}$ in.) and glue in place. Join the shoulder seams then turn in the neck, arm-hole and lower edges 3 mm ($\frac{1}{8}$ in.) and glue, to neaten. Join the side seams. Sew hooks and thread loops to the back opening edges. (See fig. 24.)

To make the skirt

Cut two skirt pieces from felt as directed on pattern 12q. Lap one centre edge of one piece 6 mm ($\frac{1}{4}$ in.) over the centre edge of the other piece and glue it in place. Machine stitch, using contrasting thread, along the lower edge then up the overlapped centre edges. Sew small beads for 'buttons' to the centre stitching. Overlap the remaining centre edges 6 mm ($\frac{1}{4}$ in.) and machine stitch them together half way up from the hem. Sew a snap fastener to the waist edges. Position the skirt on the doll so that the snap fasten-ing is at the centre back. (See fig. 24.)

Left **Figure 24** Mary in striped sweater and skirt

To make the beach smock and shorts

For the yoke of the smock cut an 18 cm (7 in.) length of 2.5 cm (1 in.) wide lace edging. Fold the strip in half along the length and press, forming a 1.3 cm ($\frac{1}{2}$ in.) wide strip. Turn in the raw edges at the ends of the strip 6 mm ($\frac{1}{4}$ in.) and sew in place. Using the yoke pattern 12r as a guide, form the strip into a rectangular shape mitring and sewing the corners in place. For the smock top use the nightdress body pattern (12f) trimming it at the upper and lower edges indicated. Cut two smock top pieces from fabric. Cut one of the pieces in half along the centre fold line for the centre back opening of the smock. Join the front to the back pieces at the side seams. Turn in the armhole edges 3 mm ($\frac{1}{8}$ in.) and glue. Sew lace edging, folded in half as for the yoke, to the lower edge of the smock then turn in the centre back edges 3 mm ($\frac{1}{8}$ in.) and glue.

Gather the upper edges of the front and backs slightly, lap the front and back edges of the yoke 6 mm ($\frac{1}{4}$ in.) over these gathered edges then sew them to the inside of the yoke. Sew a hook and thread loop to the centre back edges of the yoke.

Cut out the shorts using the panties pattern (12d). Turn in the leg edges 3 mm ($\frac{1}{8}$ in.) and glue. Join one side seam then hem the upper edge taking a 6 mm ($\frac{1}{4}$ in.) turning. Thread elastic through the turning and knot the ends to fit the doll's waist. Join the remaining side seam and glue down the ends of the elastic. (See fig. 25.)

To make the beach hat

Cut the hat shape from thin card using pattern 12s. Bring the edges marked with arrows together and hold them in position with sticky tape. Cut a 10 cm (4 in.) square of coarsely woven fabric, spread the inside of the hat with glue and press the fabric square into the hat, stretching and pushing the fab-ric to fit smoothly onto the card. Trim the edges of the fabric to within 6 mm ($\frac{1}{4}$ in.) of the card shape. Using a needle, thread the end of a length of elastic through from the inside of the hat to the outside at the points indicated on the pattern. Knot the ends of the elastic together on the outside of the hat leaving the elastic long enough on the inside to fit under the doll's chin. Glue another square of fabric to the outside of the hat and trim the edges in the same way as for the inside of the hat. Rub the raw edges of the fabric to fray them out then trim the fringe to an even length. Glue a strip of ric-rac or trimming to the outside of the hat 6 mm ($\frac{1}{4}$ in.) from the frayed out edges. (See fig. 25.)

Figure 25 Mary in beach smock, shorts and beach hat

Figure 26 Mary in party dress and fur party cape

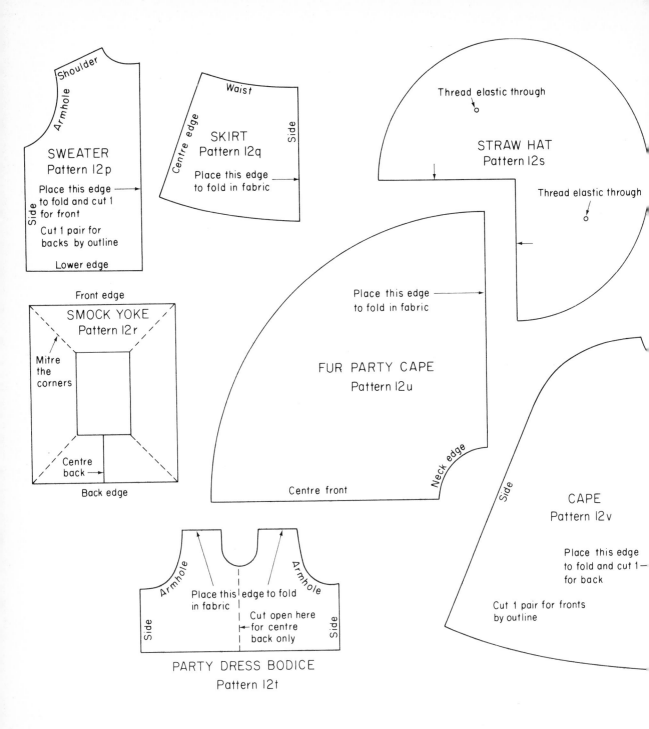

SWEATER
Pattern 12p

Shoulder

Armhole

Side

Place this edge
to fold and cut 1
for front

Cut 1 pair for
backs by outline

Lower edge

SKIRT
Pattern 12q

Waist

Centre edge

Side

Place this edge
to fold in fabric

STRAW HAT
Pattern 12s

Thread elastic through

Thread elastic through

Front edge

SMOCK YOKE
Pattern 12r

Mitre
the
corners

Centre
back

Back edge

FUR PARTY CAPE
Pattern 12u

Place this edge
to fold in fabric

Centre front

Neck edge

CAPE
Pattern 12v

Side

Place this edge
to fold and cut 1—
for back

Cut 1 pair for fronts
by outline

PARTY DRESS BODICE
Pattern 12t

Armhole

Armhole

Side

Side

Place this edge to fold
in fabric

Cut open here
for centre
back only

Page 73   **Figure 27** Mary in her short dress
Opposite   Eight small felt animals and three Victorian-style dolls
Facing page 73   Goldilocks and the Three Bears

To make the party dress

Cut out the bodice as directed on pattern 12t then cut along the dotted line shown, for the centre back opening. Turn in the armhole edges 3 mm ($\frac{1}{8}$ in.) and glue. Glue lace trimming round the neck edge to cover the raw edges then turn in the back opening edges 3 mm ($\frac{1}{8}$ in.) and glue. Join the side seams. For the skirt, cut a 10 cm by 20.5 cm (4 in. by 8 in.) strip of fabric. Join the 10 cm (4 in.) edges for 6.5 cm ($2\frac{1}{2}$ in.) then turn in and glue down the remaining raw edges of the seam for the centre back opening edges of the skirt. Gather the upper edge of the skirt and sew it to the lower edge of the bodice. Hem the lower edge of the dress and trim it with lace. Sew a ribbon bow to the front neck edge and hooks and thread loops to the back edges. (See fig. 26.)

To make the fur party cape

Cut out the cape as directed on pattern 12u. Turn in all the raw edges 3 mm ($\frac{1}{8}$ in.) and slip stitch in place. For the front neck fastening, sew a bead to each side and a loop of thread to one bead leaving another loop for fastening over the other bead (see fig. 26).

To make the short dress

Cut out two dress body pieces (pattern 12f) and two sleeve pieces (pattern 12g) trimming both patterns along the dotted lines indicated. Make the dress in the same way as the nightdress, omitting the front lace frill and sewing lace trimming to the lower edge (fig. 27).

To make the flower trimmed cape

Cut out the back and two fronts as directed on pattern 12v. Join the fronts to the back at the side seams then turn in all the raw edges 3 mm ($\frac{1}{8}$ in.) and glue. Sew a hook and thread loop to the front neck edges then glue on flower trimming as illustrated (see fig. 28).

Left **Figure 28** Mary in her flower-trimmed cape

Eight small felt animals

Above **Figure 29** Panda and rabbit

Below **Figure 30** Tiger and elephant

These quick and easy-to-make little stuffed animals are about 9 cm (3½ in.) tall. The body pattern is the same for each one and by simply varying the head shape, the ears and tails, eight different animals can be produced (see colour plate 4). The bodies are made by the stitch-around method, other seams are given in the instructions.

Materials required

Scraps of felt, trimmings, braid, fringe, and knitting wool
Kapok, cotton wool or man-made fibre stuffing
Permanent black marker pen
Adhesive

To make the body and head

These are constructed in the same way for each animal, but the instructions for each animal should also be read before starting to make any of them. Trace the body pattern 13a off the page onto thin paper then cut it out. Pin the pattern onto two layers of felt measuring about 7.5 cm by 8.5 cm (3 in. by 3¼ in.). If the animal has a tail, place one end of this between the layers of felt at the position shown on the pattern so that it will be caught in the line of stitching. Machine stitch all round close to the edge of the pattern but do not stitch across the neck edge. Cut the felt at the neck edge even with the pattern. Remove the pattern and cut out the body close to the line of stitching, taking care, if the animal has a tail, to cut the layers of felt separately at this point. Stuff the body lightly to within 2 cm (¾ in.) of the neck edge pushing the stuffing in with the point of a knitting needle.

Cut two head pieces from felt using the circular pattern 13b for all the toys except for the elephant. Slip the neck edge of the body between the head pieces as shown by the dotted lines on the head and body patterns. Now pin the head pieces together and, if ears are to be included, slip these also between the head pieces at the correct positions and pin in place. Machine stitch all round close to the edge of the head pieces for three-quarters of the way round. Now, leaving the head in position on the sewing machine, push a little stuffing inside the head then finish the machine stitching all round. Tie off and sew the thread ends into the head.

For the faces use the illustrations as a guide. Glue on small ovals, circles and triangles of felt for the facial features. Work the mouths in black thread with straight stitches except for the tiger. This is machine stitched onto one of the head pieces after

cutting it out. Note that the donkey's and elephant's faces are in profile and not facing forward like the other animals. For these two, the ears and eyes should be fixed to either side of the head. Mark the shading on all the animals' ears with marker pen as shown in the illustrations.

To make the panda

Use black felt for the body pieces and white felt for the body stripe. To position the white body stripe, cut out the body pieces a little larger all round than the pattern, then glue a white stripe on each piece cut to the size shown on the pattern (13a). Stitch the body and finish in the usual way. Use white felt for the panda's head (pattern 13b) and black for the ears (pattern 13c) enclosing the ears between the head pieces. Use black felt circles for the eye pieces and small white felt circles for the eyes as shown in the illustration (fig. 29).

To make the rabbit

Cut out and stitch the small ear shapes, shown by the dotted line on the rabbit's ear pattern (13d), to the larger ear pieces, before placing the ears between the head pieces. Make a small ball of cotton wool for the tail and sew it in place after the body is stuffed (fig. 29).

To make the tiger

Use a twist of wool with a knot tied in the end for the tail. Enclose the ears (pattern 13e) between the head pieces. When the tiger is completed mark on the stripes with black pen as shown in the illustration (fig. 30).

To make the elephant

Use a small twist of wool for the tail. Cut the head pieces using the elephant's head pattern 13f. Machine stitch round the ears then glue them in position on the head as shown on pattern 13g. Catch the straight edges of the ears in position on the head with a stitch or two. Glue a scrap of fancy braid across the elephant's back (fig. 30).

To make the donkey

Use a few strands of teased out fringe for the tail. Clip a length of fringe quite short for the mane and glue it in place after the head has been stitched. Make a line of stitching all round the ears (using pattern 13h) then sew the lower edges of the ears to the head. Glue a scrap of fancy braid over the donkey's back for a saddle (fig. 31).

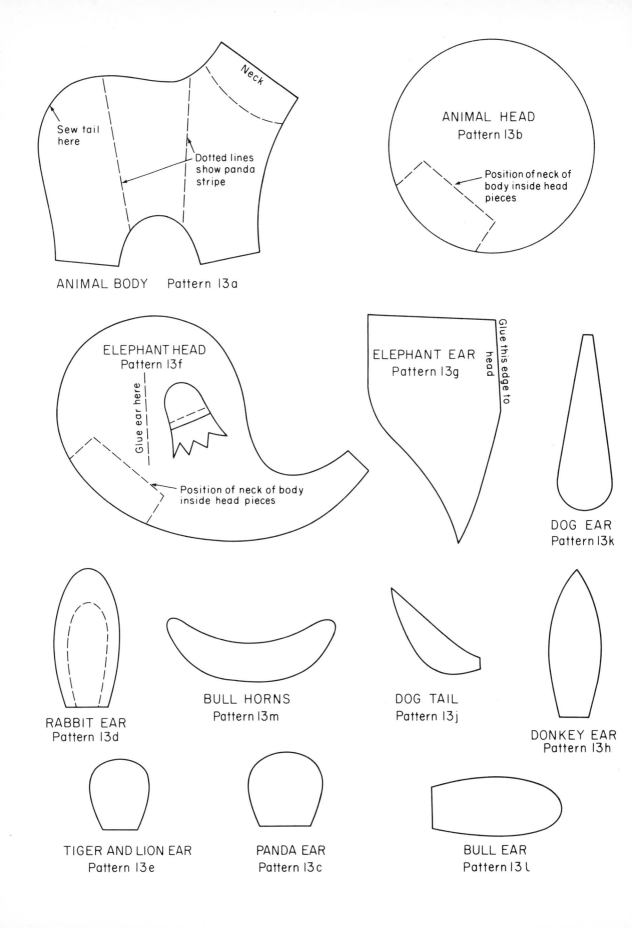

Sew tail here

Dotted lines show panda stripe

Neck

ANIMAL BODY   Pattern 13a

ANIMAL HEAD
Pattern 13b

Position of neck of body inside head pieces

ELEPHANT HEAD
Pattern 13f

Glue ear here

Position of neck of body inside head pieces

ELEPHANT EAR
Pattern 13g

Glue this edge to head

DOG EAR
Pattern 13k

RABBIT EAR
Pattern 13d

BULL HORNS
Pattern 13m

DOG TAIL
Pattern 13j

DONKEY EAR
Pattern 13h

TIGER AND LION EAR
Pattern 13e

PANDA EAR
Pattern 13c

BULL EAR
Pattern 13l

To make the lion

Use a twist of wool with a knot tied in the end for the tail. For the lion's mane glue on a piece of trimming gathered slightly to fit around the face. Glue on the ears (pattern 13e) in front of the mane (fig. 31).

To make the bull

Make the tail from a twist of wool with a knot in the end. Enclose the ears (using pattern 13l) between the head pieces at the angle shown in the illustration (fig. 32). Cut the horns piece (pattern 13m)

from two layers of felt glued together. Wrap a strand of wool, to match the tail, around the centre of the horns before gluing and sewing it in place.

To make the dog

Cut the tail and ears from two layers of felt glued together, using patterns 13j and k. Machine stitch around the edges of the ears and tail. Glue, then sew the top edges of the ears in place as shown in the illustration (fig. 32). Stick a bit of trimming round the dog's neck for a collar.

Above **Figure 31** Donkey and lion

Below **Figure 32** Dog and bull

Honey bees mobile

Here is a simple but pretty mobile to make for next to nothing (fig. 33). The bees, measuring about 2.5 cm (1 in.) in length, are made from scraps of felt with net fabric for their wings. Yellow card is used for the honeycombs and these are suspended along with the bees, from small twigs.

Materials required

A few small twigs

Pink paper tissue for the blossoms on the twigs

Thin yellow card and yellow Cellophane for the honeycombs

Scraps of gold-coloured felt, white net fabric, black thread and cotton wool, for the bees

Red and black marker pens

Transparent nylon sewing thread

Adhesive

To make the honeycombs

Cut one honeycomb section from card using pattern 14a. Using the point of a darning needle against a ruler, scribe the strip of card across the width at the positions shown by the dotted lines on the pattern. Fold the card back along the scribed lines then overlap and glue the end sections as indicated on the pattern. Make several more honeycomb sections and glue them together in groups as shown in the illustration. If desired, a honey-filled effect can be obtained by sticking on yellow Cellophane. Spread the edges of a group of honeycomb sections with glue, then place the group on a piece of Cellophane. When the glue is dry, cut the edges of the Cellophane even with the card shapes.

To make a bee

Cut the body from felt using pattern 14b. Run a strong gathering thread round close to the edge. Stuff the centre of the circle with cotton wool and pull up the gathers tightly coaxing the bee into an oval shape. Fasten off the thread. Using black marker pen, mark on four stripes around the oval body, leaving one end of the bee unstriped for the face. Mark on two black dots for eyes and a smaller dot for the nose, then a red dot for the mouth. Using black thread, work a loop of thread above each eye for a feeler.

Cut two wings from white net fabric using pattern 14c. Spread a little glue along the straight edges, gather these edges up between the fingers and glue one to each side of the bee.

To make the blossoms

Cut circles of paper tissue to the size shown on pattern 14d. Put a dab of glue in the centre of each circle and twist each one round the glued centre to gather up. Stick the blossoms on the twigs as illustrated.

To assemble the mobile

It is easiest to begin with the top twig. The one illustrated is about 25.5 cm (10 in.) long. Using the transparent nylon thread, attach a length to each bee, group of honeycombs and twig. See the illustration as a guide to assembling, and when suspending each item, find the centre of balance each time so that all the units will move freely without knocking against each other.

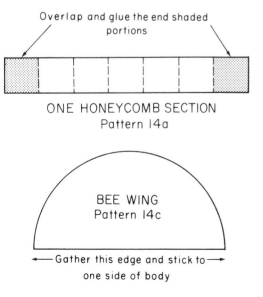

Overlap and glue the end shaded portions

ONE HONEYCOMB SECTION
Pattern 14a

BEE WING
Pattern 14c

←— Gather this edge and stick to —→
one side of body

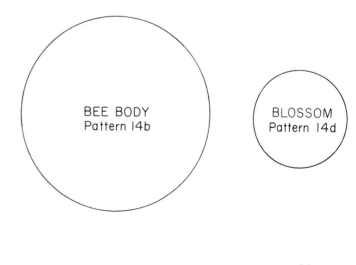

BEE BODY
Pattern 14b

BLOSSOM
Pattern 14d

Bean bag bunnies

Figure 34 Bean bag bunnies

These floppy bunnies are only 11 cm (4¼ in.) high (fig. 34). They are made from fleecy fabric and filled with dried lentils. Rice or pearl barley can be used instead of lentils, but remember to remove any of these dried fillings before washing the bunnies. The little lace-trimmed baskets are made from plastic lids off discarded aerosol cans, such as air fresheners. Alternatively, plastic yoghurt cartons can be used by cutting them down to the sizes given in the instructions. The bunnies are made by the stitch-around method and the outlines on the body and head patterns are the actual stitching lines.

Materials required for the bunnies

Scraps of fleecy fabric and black felt
Red and black thread
Narrow ribbon
About 28 grammes (1 oz) of lentils for each bunny
Lipstick for colouring the cheeks, ears and tail
Adhesive

To make a bunny

Trace the patterns 15a, b and c off the page onto thin paper. Cut out the paper patterns. Pin the body pattern 15a onto two layers of fleece having the right sides together. Machine stitch all round close to the edge of the pattern, leaving a gap in the stitching as indicated on the pattern. Remove the pattern and cut out the body about 3 mm (⅛ in.) from the stitching line. Turn the body right side out and fill it about three-quarters full with lentils, using a small funnel shape made from paper to do this easily. Turn in the raw edges and ladder stitch the opening. Turn the body upside down shaking the lentils out of the feet to leave only a few in the toe of each foot. Work small running stitches through both thicknesses of fabric where the feet join the body as indicated by the dotted lines on the pattern. Turn the feet up at right angles to the body and ladder stitch them in position as shown by the dotted lines marked 'ladder stitch' on the pattern. Bring the arms forward to the centre front of the body, folding them on the lines shown on the pattern, then ladder stitch them to the body as shown on the pattern.

Pin the head pattern 15b onto two layers of fleece, then stitch, and cut out in the same way as for the body. Turn the head right side out, using the knob end of a small knitting needle to turn the ears easily. Make small running stitches across the base of each ear. Fill the head with lentils and then turn in the raw edges and ladder stitch the opening.

Work small straight stitches for the eyelashes using black thread and sew three stitches around the end of each foot as shown in the illustration, also using black thread.

Work a few tiny stitches for the nose and a single stitch for the mouth using red thread. Twist a paper tissue to a point and apply a little lipstick to each cheek with the point, then smooth the colour into the fleecy fabric by rubbing with tissue. Colour the lower part of the ears at the front in the same way. Cut two circles of black felt for the eyes to the size shown on the head pattern, then stick them in place.

Cut the tail from fleecy fabric using pattern 15c. Run a gathering thread round the edge of the circle, put a few lentils in the centre then pull up the gathers and fasten off the thread. Ladder stitch the tail to the back of the bunny at the position shown on the body pattern. Colour the tail with lipstick.

Make a tiny bow of ribbon and sew it to the base of the ears as shown in the illustration. Place the back of the head over the front of the body matching points A and B. Catch in place at these positions with a few stitches.

Materials required for the baskets

Plastic lids from aerosol cans, about 5.5 cm (2¼ in.) diameter by 4 cm (1½ in.) deep
Small pieces of fabric, ribbon, and lace trimming
A strip of plastic cut off a washing-up liquid bottle, for the basket handle
Adhesive

To make a basket

Cut an 18 cm (7 in.) diameter circle of fabric and stick the top of the lid to the centre of the fabric circle. Spread glue all round the outside of the lid and pull the fabric circle up tightly all round, creasing and pleating the fabric onto the side of the lid as neatly as possible. Trim off the excess fabric leaving only about 1 cm (⅜ in.) extra extending above the rim of the lid. Turn this excess to the inside of the lid and stick down.

For the basket handle cut a 1 cm by 20 cm (⅜ in. by 7¾ in.) strip of plastic off the washing-up liquid bottle. Cover this with a strip of fabric, sticking it in place. Spread the ends of the handle with glue and place about 5 mm (¼ in.) inside the top edge of the basket. Sew these ends in place with a few stitches taken through the lid using a thin needle which should pierce the plastic fairly easily. Stick a strip of lace trimming round the outside of the basket as

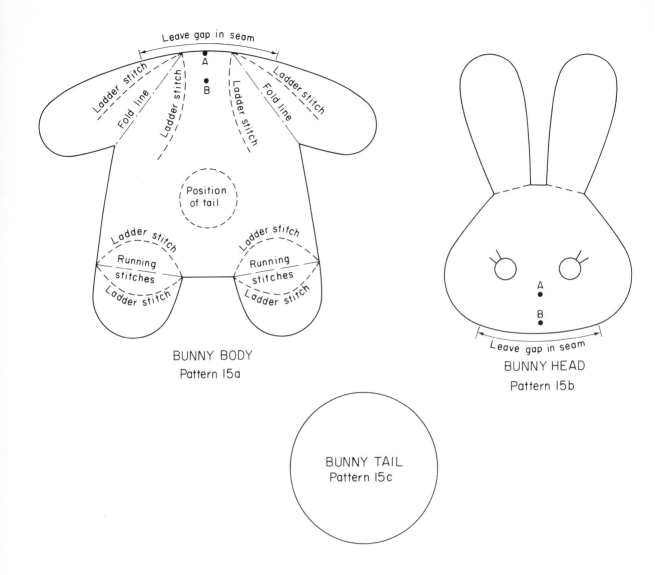

BUNNY BODY
Pattern 15a

BUNNY HEAD
Pattern 15b

BUNNY TAIL
Pattern 15c

shown in the illustration and also round the inside
to cover the raw edges of the fabric. Tie a ribbon bow
round the handle of the basket.

84

Bagatelle

Figure 35 Bagatelle

A transparent plastic cheese-spread box, measuring almost 7.5 cm (3 in.) in diameter, is used for this toy, but any kind of container which has a clear plastic top could be used. A suitable picture, cut from a greetings card, and a few small round beads are also required. In the greetings card used for the toy illustrated (fig. 35), small holes are made at the positions of the baubles on the Christmas tree, into which the small gold beads are to be rolled.

Materials required
A transparent plastic cheese-spread box
Scraps of card, braid, felt and trimmings
A few small round beads
A suitable picture from a greetings card
Adhesive

To make the bagatelle
Cut a picture to fit inside the box base. To make the holes, pierce the picture with a darning needle at the chosen positions. Now carefully push through the point of a pencil to make the holes large enough to hold the beads. Glue down the resulting rough ends of paper around each hole on the reverse side of the picture, to neaten.

Cut a circle of card the same size as the picture, place the picture over it right side up, and mark the positions of the holes onto the card circle. Using scissors, cut out the holes as marked on the circle of card, making them a little larger. Glue the card circle and the picture together. Cut another circle of card to the same size and glue it to the card side of the picture. Glue the picture inside the box base.

Put the same number of beads as there are holes inside the box. Spread glue round the top edge of the box, then put on the lid.

Glue a circle of felt to the base of the box. Glue braid or trimming round the side of the box, noting that if the braid is wider than the box side it can be turned over and glued onto the top as shown in the illustration.

Four glove puppets – the story of the three little pigs

Figure 36 Four glove puppets – the story of the three little pigs. 'The third and wisest little pig built a house of bricks, and no matter how much the wolf huffed and puffed, he could not blow it down'

Here is a complete set of toys for a puppet play (fig. 36). The puppets measure about 30 cm (12 in.) in height and they are just the right size for small hands. The little pigs' heads and hands are made from pink felt, and each is dressed in a different coloured costume, with a jaunty white sailor collar and hat. The ferocious wolf is made from brown fur fabric. There are also instructions for making the little houses which the pigs built, one of straw, one of twigs and the last one of bricks. The houses are flat shapes cut from cardboard and covered with fabric, and they have strong cardboard handles for holding them up level with the stage. Each little pig can peep out of his window, then, as the wolf huffs and puffs, the houses can be toppled over sideways disappearing below stage level. The brick house of course is not blown over. It has a chimney and at the end of the story the wolf can climb up the side of the house then disappear down the back of the chimney. On the felt and fur fabric pieces, the outline is the actual stitching line and the stitch-around method is used unless otherwise stated. For other pieces the seam allowances and turnings are given in the instructions.

Materials required for the three little pigs

Small pieces of pink felt for the hands and heads
Scraps of deep pink and black felt, black marker pen, black thread and pink lipstick, for the facial features
Thin card and sticky tape, for the neck tubes
Small pieces of fabrics, ribbon, narrow braid and white felt, for the clothes
Kapok, cotton wool or man-made fibre stuffing
Adhesive

To make a little pig

Trace the head pattern 16a off the page using thin paper. Cut out the pattern and pin it onto two layers of pink felt. Machine stitch all round close to the edge of the pattern leaving the neck edges open, and a gap in the seam at the top of the head as shown on the pattern. Trim off the felt close to the pattern at the neck edge, then remove the pattern and cut out the head close to the stitching. Turn the head right side out. Cut a 6 cm ($2\frac{3}{8}$ in.) square of thin card. Roll it up into a tube, overlapping the edges as necessary to fit the child's forefinger loosely, then secure the card edges in place with sticky tape. Cover one end of the tube with sticky tape to seal it, then push this end just inside the neck edge of the head. Spread glue round the outside of the opposite end of the tube covering about 1 cm ($\frac{3}{8}$ in.), then

push the tube right inside the head, having the glued end of the tube even with the neck edge of the head. Press the neck edge of the head firmly onto the glued part of the tube. Run a gathering thread round the neck as shown by the dotted line on the pattern, pull up the gathers tightly against the tube and fasten off.

Stuff the head firmly through the gap in the top of the head taking care to pack the stuffing evenly around the cardboard tube. Slip stitch the gap in the seam. For the fringe of hair cut a 3 cm by 6 cm ($1\frac{1}{4}$ in. by $2\frac{3}{8}$ in.) strip of pink felt. Fold it in half and stick the 3 cm ($1\frac{1}{4}$ in.) edges together. Now cut several times through the folded edge to make loops, leaving about 6 mm ($\frac{1}{4}$ in.) uncut at the glued edge. Stick this glued edge to the seam along the centre top of the head having the loops hanging down over the little pig's face.

Cut two ears from pink felt using pattern 16b. Colour the pointed ends of the ears by rubbing in a little lipstick with a finger tip. Place the lower edge of each ear along the head seam positioning the ears on either side of the fringe piece and having the pointed ends hanging down the back of the little pig's head. Oversew the lower edges of the ears in place. Now bring the pointed ends of the ears over, to hang down the face at each side as shown in the illustration. Hold the ears in this position with a dab of glue.

Cut the nose from deep pink felt to the size shown on the head pattern (16a). Mark on the nostrils with marker pen. Cut the eyes from black felt to the size shown. Place all these features on the face then mark the position of the eyebrows and mouth on the face as shown on the pattern. Work the mouth and eyebrows in black thread with small stitches then glue the eyes and nose on the face. Colour the cheeks with lipstick.

Trace the hat pattern 16c off the page onto thin paper. Cut out the pattern and pin it onto two layers of white felt. Stitch around the top curved edge close to the pattern, leaving the lower edges open. Trim off the felt even with the paper pattern at the lower edge. Remove the pattern and cut out the hat close to the stitching. Turn right side out then stretch the crown of the hat with the fingers to make a nice rounded shape. Machine stitch round and round the lower part of the hat up to the dotted line shown on the pattern. Stuff the crown of the hat, place it on the little pig's head and sew it to the head all round at the position of the dotted line. Turn up the lower edge of the hat for the brim.

Cut two body pieces from fabric using pattern 16d.

Figure 37 The three little pigs with sailor collars

Join the side edges taking 6 mm (¼ in.) seams and leaving a gap at the top of each seam as shown on the pattern. Join the top edges taking a 6 mm (¼ in.) seam and leaving a gap at the centre of the seam as shown on the pattern. Make a narrow hem on the lower edge and leave the body wrong side out.

Trace the little pig's hand pattern 16e off the page onto thin paper. Cut out the pattern and pin it onto two layers of pink felt. Stitch all round close to the pattern leaving the straight edges open. Trim off the felt at the straight edges even with the pattern. Remove the pattern and cut out the hand close to the stitching then turn right side out.

Slip the hand inside the gap at one side of the body until the raw edges of the body and straight edges of the hand are even. Back stitch the edges of the hand in place taking a 6 mm (¼ in.) seam. Make and sew on the other hand in the same way then turn the body right side out. Turn in the raw edges

of the body at the neck and run round a gathering thread. Slip the neck edge of the little pig's head inside the gathers and pull up and fasten off the gathers at the position of the gathering thread on the neck. Sew the gathered edge of the body to the neck all round.

Cut the front collar piece from striped fabric using pattern 16f. Turn in the upper edge a little and stick down, to neaten. Glue this piece to the centre front of the little pig's body just below the chin.

Cut the collar from white felt using pattern 16g. Stitch narrow braid to the collar at the position of the dotted line on the pattern. Place the collar around the little pig's neck and glue the centre front points to the lower edge of the striped front collar piece. Make a small ribbon bow and stick it to the centre front points of the collar. Make the other two little pigs in the same way using different coloured fabrics for the body pieces (see fig. 37).

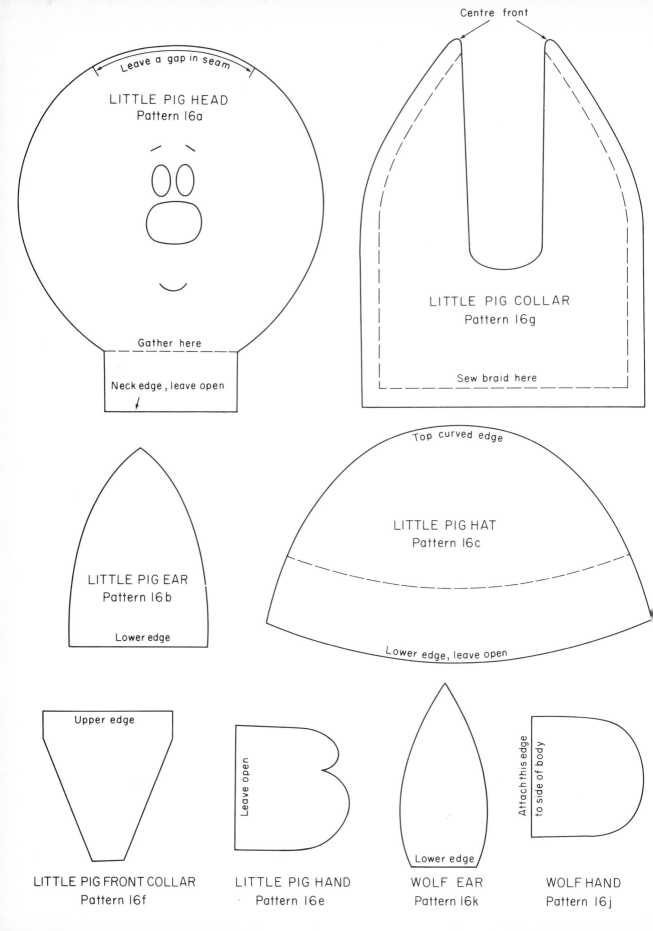

LITTLE PIG HEAD
Pattern 16a

Leave a gap in seam

Gather here

Neck edge, leave open

Centre front

LITTLE PIG COLLAR
Pattern 16g

Sew braid here

LITTLE PIG EAR
Pattern 16b

Lower edge

Top curved edge

LITTLE PIG HAT
Pattern 16c

Lower edge, leave open

Upper edge

LITTLE PIG FRONT COLLAR
Pattern 16f

Leave open

LITTLE PIG HAND
Pattern 16e

Lower edge

WOLF EAR
Pattern 16k

Attach this edge
to side of body

WOLF HAND
Pattern 16j

Top edge

Leave a gap in seam for neck edge

Leave a gap in seam for
inserting little pig's hand

Leave a gap in seam for
inserting little pig's hand

Side edge

Side egde

LITTLE PIG AND WOLF BODY PATTERN
Pattern 16d

Lower edge

Materials required for the wolf

Small pieces of dark brown fur fabric
Scraps of red, green, dark brown, and black felt
A small dome-shaped black button for the nose
Thin card and sticky tape for the neck tube
Adhesive

To make the wolf

Trace the head pattern 16h off the page onto thin paper. Cut out the paper pattern and pin it onto two layers of fur fabric having the right sides of the fabric together. Now make the head and insert the card tube in the same way as for the little pig.

Trace the body pattern (16d) off the page onto thin paper and cut it out. Trace the wolf's hand pattern 16j off the page twice onto thin paper and cut out. Place a hand pattern at each side of the body pattern at the top as shown in diagram 3, then stick in this position with bits of sticky tape.

Pin this body pattern complete with the hands onto two layers of fur fabric having the right sides of the fabric together. Stitch all round close to the pattern leaving the lower edges open and a gap in the centre of the top edge for the neck, as shown on the pattern. Cut the lower edges of the fabric even with the pattern. Remove the pattern, cut out the wolf close to the stitching, then turn right side out. Hem the lower edge. Attach the body to the wolf's head in the same way as for the little pig.

Cut two ears from brown felt using pattern 16k. Fold the ears in half at the lower edges then sew these folded edges in position as shown on the head pattern. Cut two eye pieces from red felt using the largest eye shape on the head pattern (16h), cut two from green felt using the smaller shape and two from black felt using the smallest shape. Glue the eye pieces together, then stick the eyes in position on the wolf's head. Sew on the button for the nose.

Materials required for the houses

Corrugated reinforced cardboard (cut from grocery
  boxes)
Strong card for the handles
Oddments of suitable fabrics (eg plain red for the
  brick house, coarsely woven yellow or fawn for
  the straw house and brown for the twig house)
Scraps of braids, trimming, lace and felt
Two buttons for doorknobs
Adhesive

To make the basic house

For each house cut a 28cm (11 in.) square of card. Shape the roof and cut out the window as shown in the diagram 4. Cover each house wall with fabric using the fabrics as given in the instructions which follow for each individual house. Leave the piece of fabric large enough all round to turn over and stick the raw edges to the wrong side of the card. Cut a hole in the fabric at the position of the window leaving enough fabric for turning the raw edges to the wrong side. Clip the fabric at the corners then turn and stick it to the wrong side. Cover the roof in the same way, lapping the lower edge of the roof slightly over the wall fabric. Make a handle by gluing together several 3 cm by 20 cm (1¼ in. by 8 in.) strips of strong card. Cover the handle with paper then stick it securely to the centre back of the house as shown in diagram 4.

To make the straw house

Use loosely woven fabric and if desired pull threads out of the fabric to make a more open texture. Fringe out the fabric used for the roof at the lower edge to resemble a thatched roof. Cut out the door to the size given in diagram 4. Make a loop of string for the door handle and thread it through the door, then glue the door in place. Glue a strip of the same fabric as the door beneath the window for a window sill.

To make the twig house

Make in the same way as the straw house using closer woven brown fabric. Make the door from striped fabric then cut out and stick on cross pieces to look like wooden bars. Stick on a button for a doorknob.

To make the brick house

After covering the wall with red fabric use a ruler and black marker pen to mark on the bricks. Make and stick on a brick chimney using a 6.5 cm by 7.5 cm (2½ in. by 3 in.) piece of card as shown in the diagram. Glue strips of shoe lace or braid to the back of the window for the window frame pieces then stick on strips of lace for lace curtains. Stick on the door piece then glue braid round the door and under the window. Cut a small felt keyhole and a letter box then a felt strip for a doorstep, and glue them all in place. Finally, stick on a button for the doorknob.

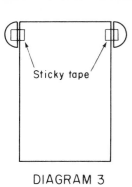

DIAGRAM 3

How to attach wolf's hands
to sides of body pattern

Sticky tape

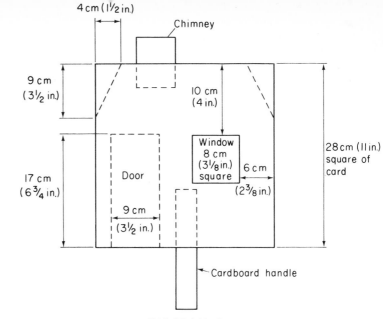

4 cm (1½ in.)

Chimney

9 cm
(3½ in.)

10 cm
(4 in.)

28 cm (11 in.)
square of
card

Window
8 cm
(3⅛ in.)
square

6 cm
(2⅜ in.)

17 cm
(6¾ in.)

Door

9 cm
(3½ in.)

Cardboard handle

DIAGRAM 4

How to cut card for each house. Make
a chimney for the brick house only
and stick it behind the roof.

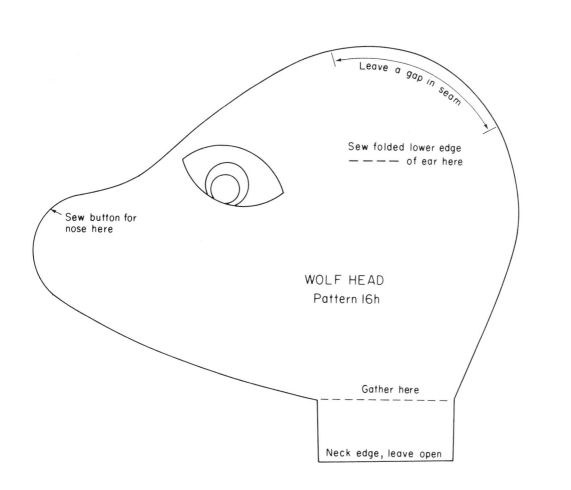

Leave a gap in seam

Sew folded lower edge
– – – – of ear here

Sew button for
nose here

WOLF HEAD
Pattern 16h

Gather here

Neck edge, leave open

Three Victorian-style dolls

Figure 38 The lady

These pretty dolls measuring 19 cm (7½ in.) in height are very easy to make (see colour plate 5). A simple cone shape of either stiff interlining fabric or card is used for the basic body shape and the head and hands are made from a table-tennis ball. Two of the dolls are purely ornamental, dressed as a lady and a flower seller. The third doll, wearing a maid's apron and mob cap, is a dressmaker's companion, holding all the most useful sewing items for general needlework. Seams and turnings are given in the instructions.

Materials required for the lady doll
Stiff interlining fabric or thin card
Table-tennis ball
One pipe cleaner
Scraps of fabrics, lace, trimmings and card
Cotton wool for stuffing
Black permanent marker pen and red pencil
Adhesive

To make the lady doll
Trace the cone pattern 17a off the page onto a piece of thin folded paper, placing the fold in the paper against the line indicated on the pattern. Cut out the pattern and open up to give the full sized semi-circular shape. Cut this piece from interlining or card, then spread glue round the edges on one side only and place it on a piece of fabric. Cut out the fabric 6 mm (¼ in.) larger all round than the semi-circle. Turn and stick the extra fabric to the wrong side of the semi-circle. Bend the semi-circle into a cone shape lapping the back edges as shown by the dotted line on the pattern. Glue the edges in this position. Glue lace trimming round the lower part of the cone as shown in the illustration (fig. 38).

For the head take the table-tennis ball and, using scissors, carefully cut around the ball as shown in diagram 5, about 3 mm (⅛ in.) above the seam line which goes round the centre of the ball. Put the larger portion on one side to be used later for the doll's head.

Trace the hand pattern 17b off the page then cut it out. Draw round the hand shape onto the smaller portion of the table tennis ball then cut it out. Reverse the pattern and cut another hand thus making a pair. If desired the hands can be cut into separate fingers rounding off the finger tips as shown on the pattern.

For the arms take the pipe cleaner and glue a hand to each end as shown in diagram 6. Pad out the pipe cleaner by wrapping a little cotton wool round it leaving the centre of the pipe cleaner uncovered.

For the sleeves cut a 5 cm by 16.5 cm (2 in. by 6½ in.) strip of fabric to match the body fabric. Overlap the long edges of the strip 3 mm (⅛ in.) and glue to form a tube. Slip the pipe cleaner arms piece through the tube. Spread glue on the wrist edges of the fabric and press it on to the wrist edges of the hands gathering up the fullness to fit. Glue a bit of lace trimming on each wrist to cover the raw edges.

Glue the centre of the arms piece to the cone at the back about 1.3 cm (½ in.) down from the top point, holding the arms piece in place with pins until the glue dries. Bend the arms round the cone towards the front of the doll. Glue lace trimming to match the lower edge trimming, round the top point of the cone.

Take the portion of the table-tennis ball that was laid aside for the head. Cut out a 9 mm (⅜ in.) diameter hole opposite the cut edge, for the neck. Using an ordinary pencil mark on the hairline at each side of the face and the eyes, nose and mouth. Colour the head all over as far as the hairline using black marker pen, then draw on little tendrils of hair at the hairline as illustrated. Colour the eyes black, then draw on the nose and mouth using red pencil. Colour the cheeks with red pencil then smooth the colour into the cheeks by rubbing with a moistened finger tip.

Fix the head in position on top of the cone, spreading glue on the top point of the cone and round the neck edge of the head. Spread a little extra glue inside the head at the neck edge then leave to dry thoroughly.

For the hat brim cut a 7 cm (2¾ in.) diameter circle of card. Glue this circle to the centre of a 13 cm (5 in.) diameter circle of fabric. Run a gathering thread round the edge of the fabric circle, spread the card circle with glue then pull up the gathers tightly and fasten off. For the crown of the hat cut a 10 cm (4 in.) diameter circle of fabric. Run a gathering thread round the edge then pull up the gathers, at the same time stuffing the centre of the circle firmly with cotton wool. Fasten off the thread. Spread glue on the gathered side of the crown of the hat and press this onto the centre of the hat brim using pins to hold it firmly in place until the glue dries. Glue the hat brim to the top of the doll's head then decorate the hat with rosettes of ribbon and lace.

For the shawl cut a 24 cm (9½ in.) length of broad ribbon, fray out the ends to make a fringe, then glue the shawl in place on the doll as illustrated (fig. 38).

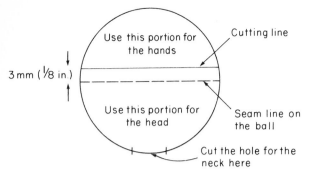

DIAGRAM 5 How to cut the table tennis ball for the doll's head

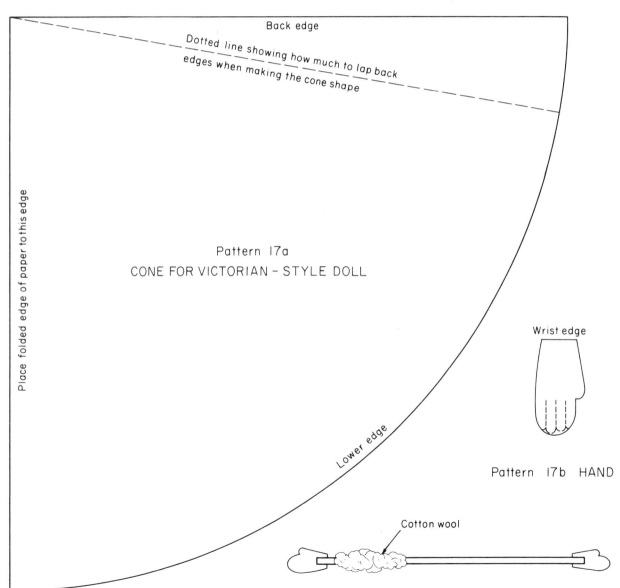

Place folded edge of paper to this edge

Back edge

Dotted line showing how much to lap back edges when making the cone shape

Pattern 17a
CONE FOR VICTORIAN – STYLE DOLL

Lower edge

Wrist edge

Pattern 17b HAND

Cotton wool

DIAGRAM 6 Hands glued in place on the pipe cleaner

Materials required for the flower seller doll

The same materials as for the lady doll plus the items
listed below

A matchbox tray
Dried or artificial flowers
Small feathers
Braid for the flower basket

To make the flower seller doll

Make in the same way as for the lady doll with the
following exceptions. To give the effect of a lace
blouse, glue 5 cm (2 in.) wide lace trimming around
the top of the cone and also use this type of lace for
the sleeves.

For the shawl cut a 14 cm (5½ in.) square of
fabric. Fray out round the edges to make a fringe.
Fold the shawl corner to corner and glue it on the
doll as shown in the illustration (fig. 39).

For the flower basket, cut about 6 mm (¼ in.)
off the upper edge of the matchbox tray. Glue
braid round the sides of the tray. For the basket
handle cut a 7.5 cm (3 in.) length of braid, fold it in
half along the length and glue. Glue the handle in
position across the basket. Stick flowers in the basket,
then glue the basket over one of the doll's arms.
Glue a small bunch of flowers to the other hand.

Glue feathers and ribbon rosettes to the hat. Note
that the feathers can be curled by drawing them
carefully between the thumb and a blunt knife
blade.

Materials required for the dressmaker's companion

The same materials as for the lady doll plus the
items listed below

1.4 m (1½ yd) of narrow broderie Anglaise or other
trimming
Pins
Needles
Safety pins
Small scissors
Thimble
Small tape measure
Two reels of sewing thread

To make the dressmaker's companion

Make the cone shape, the arms and the head in the
same way as for the lady doll.

For the hat brim cut a 4.5 cm (1¾ in.) diameter
circle of card. Glue a frill of gathered trimming
round the outer edge of the card circle on both
sides. Make the crown of the hat and glue it in
place as for the lady doll then glue the hat to the
doll's head.

98

For the apron cut a 13 cm (5 in.) square of fabric.
Hem and sew trimming to one edge then turn this
edge up 4 cm (1½ in.) to form a pocket having the
right side of the fabric outside. Turn in and stitch
3 mm (⅛ in.) hems on the side edges of the apron,
then sew trimming down each side and across the
lower folded edge of the pocket. Make suitable
divisions in the pocket for holding the cotton reels
etc, by stitching up the pocket from the lower edge.
Gather the upper raw edge of the apron to measure
about 7.5 cm (3 in.) then sew this gathered edge
to the centre of a 16.5 cm (6½ in.) length of trimming for the waistband. Glue the waistband round
the doll, lapping the ends at the centre back, and
easing it to fit the cone shape.

For the shoulder straps cut a 25.5 cm (10 in.)
strip of trimming. Fold it in half making a V-shape
at the fold. Glue this point to the centre front of the
apron waistband. Take the straps over the shoulders,
cross them over at the back and finally glue the ends
into loops at the centre back of the waistband. These
loops are used for slipping the scissors through (fig.
41).

Bend the arms and wrists as shown in the illustration (fig. 40) so that the hands will hold the
thimble. Glue the wrists to the apron waistband,
holding them in position with pins until the glue
dries.

Place all the sewing items on the doll as shown in
the illustrations. Use the crown of the doll's hat for
the pincushion.

Figure 41 Back view of the dressmaker's companion

Magic tortoise toy

Figure 42 Magic tortoise toy

100

The tortoise's garden is made from a cheese-spread portions cardboard box, measuring about 11 cm (4¼ in.) diameter, but any kind of small box lid could be used instead. In the garden there is a little house, a lettuce patch, a pond, paved path, flower borders and bushes. The tiny tortoise, only 2.5 cm (1 in.), has a small metal disc glued underneath so that he can be moved about the garden by sliding a magnet around beneath the box. An Eclipse button magnet is used for the toy illustrated, and this is the most suitable kind as it comes complete with a metal disc. Alternatively, any kind of magnet will do if a small metal washer is glued to the tortoise instead of the disc. Use the illustration (fig. 42) as a guide to placing all the garden features or re-arrange them if desired.

Materials required

Cheese-spread portions box

Eclipse button magnet (or other magnet plus a 1.3 cm (½ in.) diameter metal washer)

Tube about 2.5 cm (1 in.) diameter (such as a 'Smarties' container)

Scraps of trimmings, fabric, card, paper, sweet wrappings, guipure flower trimming, tights or stocking, cotton wool, cord or string, green synthetic foam sponge

Adhesive

To make the garden

Discard the cheese box lid and use only the base. To reinforce the side of the box, glue on a strip of card cut to fit around the outside. Glue trimming round the side of the box on the inside and outside, for the garden fence.

For the grass, cut a circle of green fabric or paper to fit inside the box, then glue it in place. For the pond, cut a 2 cm by 2.5 cm (¾ in. by 1 in.) oval of blue Cellophane sweet wrapping paper and stick it onto an oval of silver paper cut to the same size. Glue the pond to the grass as illustrated.

For the tortoise's house, cut a 2.5 cm (1 in.) long section (having a base at one end of the tube) from the tube then cut and trim this section along its length to make a semi-circular shape measuring about 5 cm (2 in.) around the curve. Cover the house with fabric or paper, glue trimming round the front entrance then glue the house in place on the grass. Roll up a small tube of card for a chimney, pierce a hole in the house at one side and glue the chimney in place with a wisp of cotton-wool smoke glued in the top.

For the path, cut small irregular oval pieces of paper and stick them to the grass and around the pond as shown in the illustration. Colour the grass around the path with brown marker pen.

For the lettuce patch soil cut a small piece of brown fabric or paper and glue it in place. For each lettuce cut a 3 mm by 2.5 cm (⅛ in. by 1 in.) strip of green paper. Snip one long edge of the strip into points, then spread with glue and roll up the strip easing the points outwards for the lettuce leaves. Glue the lettuces in place on the soil. Glue some guipure flowers and bits of foam sponge in place in the garden as illustrated. For safe keeping, attach the magnet to one end of a 25.5 cm (10 in.) length of cord. Thread the other end of the cord through a hole pierced in the box side behind the house, then knot the end.

To make the tortoise

For the body, cut a 2.5 cm (1 in.) diameter circle of nylon stocking or tights fabric. For the tortoise-shell effect, cut another circle from brown net stocking or tights fabric if available. Note that, alternatively, the tortoise shell markings can be made with a felt-tipped pen.

Run a gathering thread round the edge of the two circles or the single circle, put a little cotton wool in the centre then pull up the gathers and fasten off the thread.

For the head, gather and stuff a 9 mm (⅜ in.) diameter circle of stocking or tights fabric in the same way as for the body. Glue the gathered part of the head under one end of the body then stretch the head forward and upwards. Mark on tiny black dots for the eyes.

For the hat cut a 9 mm (⅜ in.) diameter circle of coloured card then cut out two slightly smaller circles of the same card and glue them on top for the crown of the hat. Glue the hat to the head.

Coat one side of the metal disc or washer with glue and allow it to dry, then glue this side securely underneath the tortoise.

Goldilocks and the three bears

Figure 43 Goldilocks and the three bears. 'Who's been sleeping in my bed' cried baby bear

The story of Goldilocks comes to life with these small stuffed toys (see colour plate 6). Father and mother bear measure about 22.5 cm (8¾ in.) in height while baby bear measures 15 cm (6 in.) (fig. 43). All the bears are made from fawn fleecy fabric. Goldilocks measures 16.5 cm (6½ in.) and she is quick to make from strips of pink stockinette sewn and stuffed into sausage shapes. These are then bound with thread to shape the neck, wrists and ankles. The tiny clothes are nearly all made from straight strips of fabric sewn directly onto the toys. One or two items of clothing are removeable, giving the toys extra play value. Patterns and instructions are also given for making baby bear's bed, using chip board for the bed ends and a strong cardboard box for the mattress. Seams and turnings are as follows, on Goldilocks and the bears 3 mm (⅛ in.) and on all the clothes 6 mm (¼ in.), unless otherwise stated. When cutting out the stockinette pieces, be sure to have the 'most stretch' in the fabric in the direction shown on the pattern pieces.

Materials required for Goldilocks

Small piece of pink stockinette
Small ball of yellow knitting wool for the hair
Kapok or man-made fibre stuffing
Scraps of fabrics and trimmings for the clothes
Black and red thread and lipstick for the facial
features

To make Goldilocks

Cut the body and head piece from stockinette using pattern 18a. Join the centre back edges. Run a gathering thread round, close to the top edge, pull up the gathers and fasten off. Turn right side out and stuff to make a sausage shape measuring about 11 cm (4¼ in.) around. Turn in the remaining raw edge and slip stitch the opening, having the centre back seam at the back of the doll. Tie a few strands of sewing thread tightly around the shape about 5 cm (2 in.) down from the gathered top edge, to make the neck. Sew the thread ends into the neck.

Cut one leg piece from stockinette using pattern 18b. Join the centre back edges. Run a gathering thread round and close to the lower edge of the leg, pull up the gathers and fasten off. Turn right side out and stuff, then turn in the remaining top raw edge and slip stitch the opening, having the seam at the centre back of the leg. Tie a strand of sewing thread round the leg about 2 cm (¾ in.) up from the lower edge to make the foot and ankle. Turn the

foot up at right angles to the leg, then ladder stitch it to the leg to hold in this position. Make the other leg in the same way, then sew the tops of the legs to the lower edge of the body.

Cut one arm piece from stockinette using pattern 18c. Join the centre back edges. Run a gathering thread round and close to the lower edge, pull up and fasten off. Turn and stuff the arm then run a gathering thread round the remaining raw edge, pull up the gathers tightly and fasten off, making sure that the arm is firmly stuffed right up to the gathers. Tie a strand of sewing thread round the arm about 1.3 cm (½ in.) from the gathered lower edge, to form the wrist. Make the other arm in the same way but do not sew the arms to the body at this stage.

For the eyes, work two tiny circles in satin stitch using black thread, about half way down the head. Work three tiny straight stitches on each eye for eyelashes. Using red thread work a small straight stitch for the nose and a small cross stitch for the mouth as shown in the illustration, Colour the cheeks by rubbing a little lipstick into the fabric. The hair is sewn on after the doll has been clothed.

To make Goldilocks' shoes

Cut two soles and two shoe uppers from felt using patterns 18d and 18e. Join the short edges of each of the upper pieces by oversewing. Oversew the lower edges of the uppers to the soles all round, matching points A. Place a shoe on each foot then slip stitch the top edges of the uppers to the feet easing the felt to fit. Cut two 3 mm (⅛ in.) wide strips of felt for the shoe straps, long enough to go around the doll's ankles. Take a strap around each ankle and sew the ends to the centre back of each shoe.

To make Goldilocks' pants

Cut a 4.5 cm by 13 cm (1¾ in. by 5 in.) strip of fabric. Turn in the long raw edges of the strip and stitch, close to the folded edges. Sew a strip of narrow lace edging to one long edge. Join the short edges of the strip. Place the pants on the doll having the seam at the centre back and the lace trimmed edge at the tops of the legs. Catch the back of the pants to the front with a few stitches between the doll's legs. Run gathering threads around the upper and lower edges of the pants, pull up the gathers to fit the doll and fasten off. Sew the waist edge of the pants to the doll.

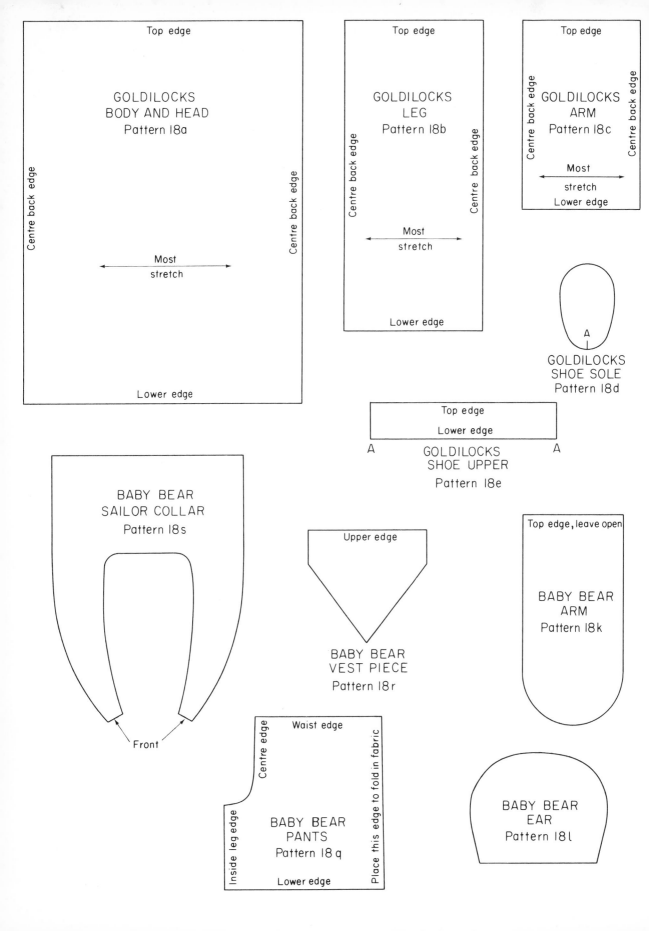

GOLDILOCKS
BODY AND HEAD
Pattern 18a

Top edge

Centre back edge

Centre back edge

Most stretch

Lower edge

GOLDILOCKS
LEG
Pattern 18b

Top edge

Centre back edge

Centre back edge

Most stretch

Lower edge

GOLDILOCKS
ARM
Pattern 18c

Top edge

Centre back edge

Centre back edge

Most stretch

Lower edge

GOLDILOCKS
SHOE SOLE
Pattern 18d

A

GOLDILOCKS
SHOE UPPER
Pattern 18e

Top edge

Lower edge

A   A

BABY BEAR
SAILOR COLLAR
Pattern 18s

Front

BABY BEAR
VEST PIECE
Pattern 18r

Upper edge

BABY BEAR
ARM
Pattern 18k

Top edge, leave open

BABY BEAR
PANTS
Pattern 18q

Centre edge

Waist edge

Inside leg edge

Lower edge

Place this edge to fold in fabric

BABY BEAR
EAR
Pattern 18l

To make Goldilocks' dress

For the dress skirt cut a 6.5 cm by 30.5 cm (2½ in. by 12 in.) strip of fabric. Make a narrow hem on one long edge of the strip and run a gathering thread along the other long edge. For the dress bodice cut a 4.5 cm by 13 cm (1¾ in. by 5 in.) strip of fabric. Sew the gathered edge of the skirt to one 13 cm (5 in.) edge of the bodice pulling up the skirt gathers to fit. Turn in the remaining 13 cm (5 in.) edge of the bodice and run a gathering thread along the folded edge. Join the remaining raw edges of the skirt and bodice then place the dress on the doll, taking it over the doll's head with the seam at the centre back. Pull up the gathers round the neck and fasten off.

For one sleeve cut a 4 cm by 7.5 cm (1½ in. by 3 in.) strip of fabric. Join the short edges of the strip then turn it right side out. Turn in the remaining raw edges. Run a gathering thread round one of the folded edges then place the top of one of the doll's arms about 6 mm (¼ in.) inside this gathered edge. Pull up the gathers to fit the arm then fasten off and sew the gathered edge to the arm. Gather the remaining sleeve edge then sew this edge in place at one side of the doll, taking the stitches through the dress fabric and into the doll. Catch the rest of the sleeve to the bodice with a few stitches. Bend the arm forward at the approximate position of the elbow, and ladder stitch a small dart in the crook of the arm to hold in place. Make the other sleeve and sew on the arm in the same way.

To make Goldilocks' apron

Cut a 25.5 cm (10 in.) long strip of lace trimming such as broderie Anglaise, about 4.5 cm (1¾ in.) in width. Gather up the strip along one long edge to measure about 10 cm (4 in.). Cut a 30.5 cm (12 in.) length of narrow tape or ribbon for the apron waistband then sew the gathered edge of the apron to the centre of the length of tape. For the shoulder straps cut two 7.5 cm (3 in.) strips of narrow trimming to match the apron, gather up one long edge of each strip to measure 6.5 cm (2½ in.). Sew the short edges of the strips to the centre front and back of the apron waistband forming the straps which pass over the doll's shoulders.

To make Goldilocks' hair

Take a few strands of knitting wool about 20.5 cm (8 in.) long. Holding on firmly to one lot of wool ends, brush and comb the other ends to tease out into fine strands. Tease out the other ends of the wool strands in the same way. Repeat this process with more lengths of wool until there is enough to cover the doll's head. Back stitch the centre of the strands to the centre parting of the head from the nape of the neck to the forehead. Stroke all the strands downwards then catch to the head all round with tiny stitches about level with the mouth. Trim the ends of the hair to an even length all round.

Materials required for the three bears

Fawn fleecy fabric 23 cm (¼ yd) by 142 cm (48 in.) wide

Scraps of black, blue and brown felt and black thread, for the facial features

Kapok or man-made fibre stuffing

Small pieces of fabrics, felt, trimmings, lace, ribbon, braid and small buttons, for the clothes

Adhesive

To make father bear

Cut out two body pieces using the large bear pattern 18f. Join them round the edges leaving a gap in the seam as shown on the pattern and following the dotted stitching lines indicated between the legs. Cut open the fabric carefully between these stitching lines. Turn the bear right side out, stuff the legs almost to the dotted stitching line shown on the pattern, then machine stitch through both body pieces at this dotted line. Stuff the head and then the body firmly, then turn in the raw edges of the opening, and slip stitch. Tie a few strands of sewing thread tightly around the neck, then sew the thread ends into the neck.

For the eyes cut two 6 mm (¼ in.) diameter circles of blue felt and two slightly smaller circles of black felt. Glue the black circles to the blue circles. Place the eyes 4.5 cm (1¾ in.) apart and half way down the face. Sew them together taking stitches from the centre of one eye, through the stuffing at the front of the face, to the other eye. Pull the thread up tightly until the eyes are about 2.5 cm (1 in.) apart, then fasten off the thread. Cut the nose from brown felt to the size shown on the pattern (18f) then sew it in place. Work the mouth in straight stitches using black thread. Cut out four large bear ear pieces using pattern 18g, join them in pairs leaving the lower edges open. Turn the ears right side out, then turn in the remaining raw edges and slip stitch, pulling the thread tightly to gather slightly. Sew the ears to the head just in front of the head seam as shown on pattern 18f.

Cut out four large bear arm pieces using pattern

Figure 44 Father bear

Figure 45 Mother bear

18h, and join them in pairs leaving the top edges open. Turn the arms right side out and stuff the lower portion only. Oversew the top raw edges of each arm together. Do not sew the arms to the body at this stage.

To make mother bear

Make in the same way as father bear but take a 6 mm ($\frac{1}{4}$ in.) seam on the body pieces instead of a 3 mm ($\frac{1}{8}$ in.) seam. Trim the seam before turning right side out. Work two small straight stitches above each eye for eyelashes, using black thread.

To make baby bear

Make in the same way as father bear using the baby bear body, arm and ear patterns 18j, k and l. Place the eyes about 3 cm ($1\frac{1}{4}$ in.) apart and pull up the thread until they are 2 cm ($\frac{3}{4}$ in.) apart. Work eyelashes as for mother bear.

To make father bear's shirt

Cut a 6.5 cm by 19 cm ($2\frac{1}{2}$ in. by $7\frac{1}{2}$ in.) strip of fabric. Join the short edges of the strip. Turn it right

side out and place on the bear taking it up over the legs and having the seam at the centre back. Turn in the neck edge and run a gathering thread around it, pull up the gathers tightly around the bear's neck and fasten off. For the collar cut a 4 cm by 15 cm ($1\frac{1}{2}$ in. by 6 in.) strip of fabric, fold it, bringing the long raw edges together, then stitch round all the raw edges leaving a gap in the seam for turning. Trim the seam, turn right side out then slip stitch the opening. Place the collar around the bear's neck and slip stitch it to the shirt having the short edges of the collar meeting at the centre front.

For one sleeve cut a 7.5 cm by 10 cm (3 in. by 4 in.) strip of fabric. Gather one of the 10 cm (4 in.) edges to measure 7.5 cm (3 in.). For the wristband cut a 2.5 cm by 7.5 cm (1 in. by 3 in.) strip of fabric. Fold it in half bringing the long edges together and having the right side of the fabric outside. Sew the long edges to the gathered edge of the sleeve. Join the 7.5 cm (3 in.) edges of the sleeve and wristband. Turn the sleeve right side out and place it over the bear's arm. Turn in the top raw edges of the sleeve and slip stitch, pulling the thread up tight,

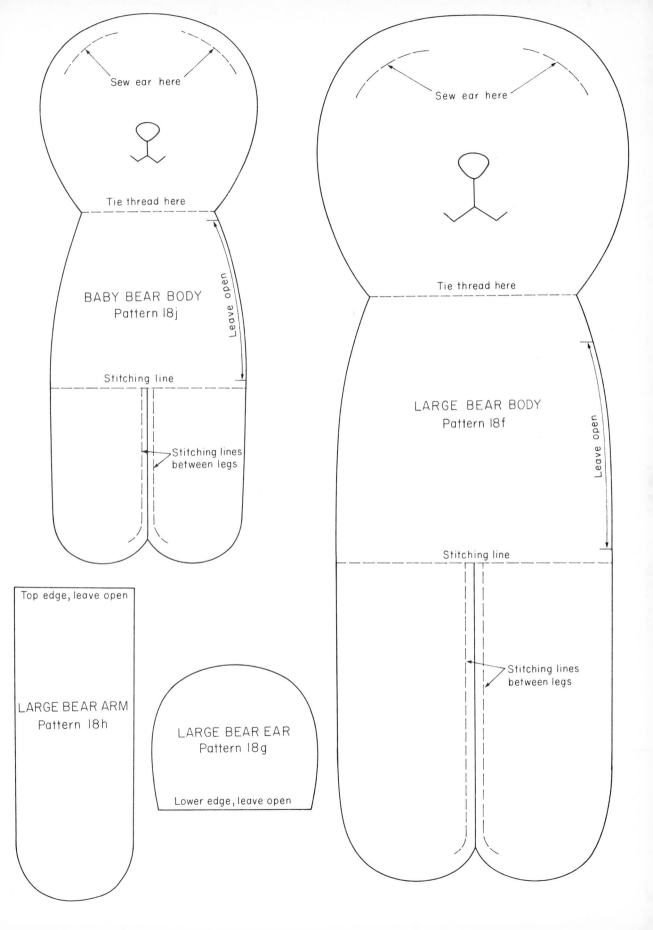

Sew ear here

Tie thread here

BABY BEAR BODY
Pattern 18j

Leave open

Stitching line

Stitching lines
between legs

Sew ear here

Tie thread here

LARGE BEAR BODY
Pattern 18f

Leave open

Stitching line

Stitching lines
between legs

Top edge, leave open

LARGE BEAR ARM
Pattern 18h

LARGE BEAR EAR
Pattern 18g

Lower edge, leave open

and at the same time catching in the top of the arm. Sew this top edge of the sleeve to one side of the bear, taking the stitches through the shirt fabric and into the bear. Make the other sleeve in the same way.

Cut a 35.5 cm (14 in.) length of narrow ribbon and wind it round the base of the shirt collar, tying it in a bow at the front. Sew small buttons down the front of the shirt.

To make father bear's pants

Cut out two pants pieces from pattern 18m, placing the edge of the pattern indicated against a fold each time. Join the pants pieces together at the centre edges then clip the seams at the curves. Bring the centre seams together and join the inside leg edges. Turn the lower edges to the wrong side and slip stitch in place. Turn the pants right side out and put them on the bear. Turn in the waist edge of the pants and slip stitch it to the shirt.

To make father bear's waistcoat

Cut the waistcoat from felt using pattern 18n, placing the edge of the pattern indicated to a fold in the felt. Fold back the lapels as shown on the pattern, then machine stitch all round the edges of the waistcoat using contrasting coloured thread. Lap the front shoulder edges 3 mm ($\frac{1}{8}$ in.) over the back shoulder edges and sew in place.

To make father bear's spectacles

Use gold gift wrapping braid for these. Cut a 10 cm (4 in.) length and bend into a 1.3 cm ($\frac{1}{2}$ in.) diameter circle at each end, then sew the ends in position. Sew the centre of the spectacles in position over the bear's nose as shown in the illustration (fig. 44).

To make mother bear's petticoat and dress

For the petticoat cut a 12 cm by 40.5 cm ($4\frac{3}{4}$ in. by 16 in.) strip of fabric. Make a narrow hem on one long edge then sew on lace trimming. Join the short edges of the strip then run a gathering thread around the remaining raw edge. Do not sew the petticoat in place on the bear at this stage.

For the dress skirt cut a 13 cm by 40.5 cm (5 in. by 16 in.) strip of fabric. Make a narrow hem on one long edge and sew on lace trimming then run a gathering thread along the other long edge. For the dress bodice cut a 5 cm by 18 cm (2 in. by 7 in.) strip of fabric. Stitch the gathered edge of the dress skirt to one 18 cm (7 in.) edge of the bodice pulling up the skirt gathers to fit. Turn in the remaining 18 cm (7 in.) edge of the bodice, sew on lace trim-

ming then run a gathering thread along this edge. Join the remaining raw edges of the skirt and bodice then turn the dress right side out. Place the petticoat inside the dress and sew the gathered raw edge to the waist edges of the dress. Place the dress on the bear taking it up over the legs and having the seam at the centre back. Pull up the gathers tightly round the bear's neck and fasten off (see fig. 45).

For one sleeve cut an 8.5 cm by 9 cm ($3\frac{1}{4}$ in. by $3\frac{1}{2}$ in.) strip of fabric. Narrowly hem and sew lace to one 9 cm ($3\frac{1}{2}$ in.) edge. Join the 8.5 cm ($3\frac{1}{4}$ in.) edges and turn right side out. Place the sleeve over the bear's arm and sew in position in the same way as for father bear. Make the other sleeve in the same way.

To make mother bear's apron

Cut a 7 cm by 9 cm ($2\frac{3}{4}$ in. by $3\frac{1}{2}$ in.) piece of fabric. Gather up one 9 cm ($3\frac{1}{2}$ in.) edge slightly. Hem and sew lace trimming to the remaining raw edges. Sew the gathered edge of the apron to the centre of a 35.5 cm (14 in.) length of tape.

To make mother bear's cape

Cut the cape from felt or other non-fray fabric using pattern 18p, placing the edge of the pattern indicated to a fold in the fabric. Stitch all round the edges of the cape using contrasting coloured thread. Sew a small button and a loop of thread to the centre front neck edges for the fastening (see fig. 43).

To make mother bear's lace cap

Cut a 30.5 cm (12 in.) length of lace trimming. Gather it up tightly along one long edge and sew it between the bear's ears. Gather up a short length of ribbon and sew this to the centre of the cap.

To make baby bear's pants

Cut out the pants pieces using baby bear's pants pattern (18q) then make in the same way as for father bear's pants. Slip stitch the waist edge of the pants to the bear.

To make baby bear's sailor blouse

Cut a 6.5 cm by 14 cm ($2\frac{1}{2}$ in. by $5\frac{1}{2}$ in.) strip of fabric. Turn in one long edge and stitch, then trim this edge by sewing on two rows of narrow braid or tape. Join the 6.5 cm ($2\frac{1}{2}$ in.) edges then turn right side out. Place the blouse on the bear taking it up over the legs and having the seam at the centre

Right **Figure 46** Baby bear

back. Turn in the remaining raw edge and run a gathering thread round it. Pull up the gathers around the bear's neck and fasten off the thread.

For one sleeve cut a 4.5 cm by 6.5 cm ($1\frac{3}{4}$ in. by $2\frac{1}{2}$ in.) strip of fabric. Hem and trim one 6.5 cm ($2\frac{1}{2}$ in.) edge in the same way as for the blouse. Join the 4.5 cm ($1\frac{3}{4}$ in.) edges then turn right side out and place the sleeve on the bear's arm. Turn in the upper sleeve edge and sew to the bear in the same way as for the other bears. Make the other sleeve in the same way.

To make baby bear's vest piece
Cut out the vest piece using pattern 18r. Turn in the upper edge and stitch. Sew this upper edge to the sailor blouse right beneath baby bear's chin, then sew all the other edges of the vest to the blouse.

To make baby bear's sailor collar
Cut the collar from white felt using pattern 18s, then work two rows of contrasting coloured stitching round the outer edges. Place the collar on the bear and join the short edges together at the centre front. Sew this front point to the lower edge of the vest piece. Make a ribbon bow and sew it to the front point of the collar (see fig. 46).

To make baby bear's bed
Use chip board for this about 1 cm ($\frac{3}{8}$ in.) in thickness. Draw the bed end shapes from pattern 18t onto the board and cut out using a coping saw or fret saw. Sandpaper to smooth and round off the edges, and cut the heart shape out of the bed head as shown on the pattern. Paint the bed ends. For the mattress use a strong cardboard carton the same width as the bed ends and about 17 cm ($6\frac{3}{4}$ in.) in length and 1.6 cm ($\frac{5}{8}$ in.) deep. Cover the mattress with fabric, then stick securely to the bed ends at the positions shown on the patterns. The mattress can be held more securely to the bed ends with a couple of small nails if desired. Make a small pillow and bed cover to complete the bed.

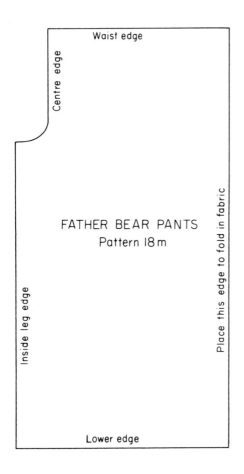

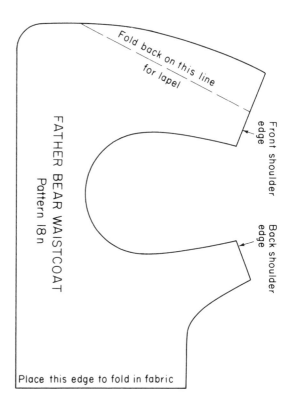

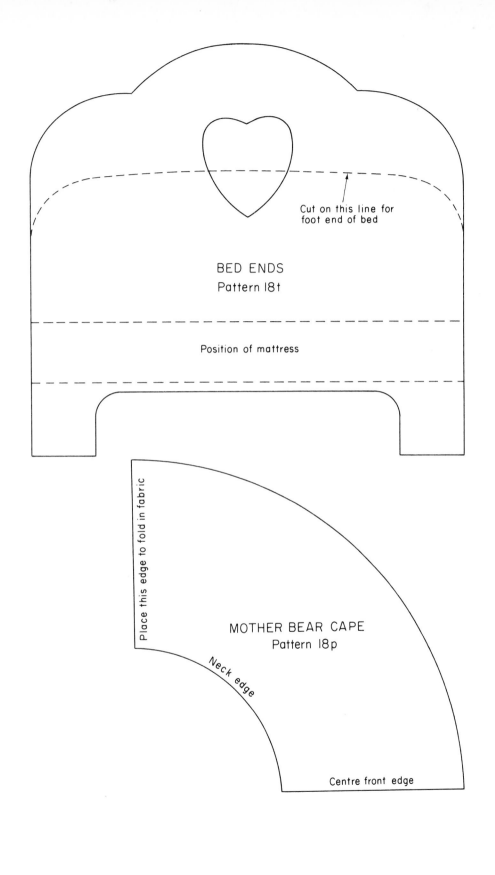

Cut on this line for
foot end of bed

BED ENDS
Pattern 18t

Position of mattress

Place this edge to fold in fabric

MOTHER BEAR CAPE
Pattern 18p

Neck edge

Centre front edge

Punch and Judy
puppet show

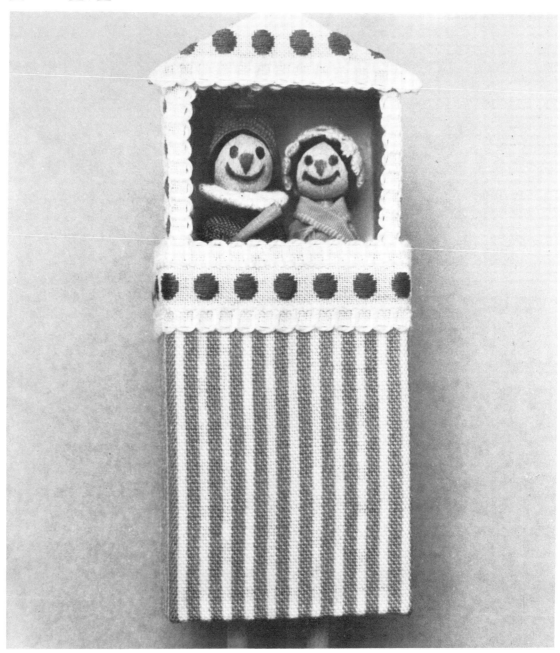

This tiny puppet show is made from an ordinary matchbox (fig. 47). Two small wooden beads and two lollipop sticks are used for the puppets on sticks. The puppets can be in full view on the 'stage' or pulled down out of sight.

Materials required

One matchbox, standard size

Scraps of braid, trimmings, fabrics, coloured paper and card

Red and black felt pens or pencils for marking on the faces

Two round lollipop sticks or two 11.5 cm (4½ in.) lengths of 3 mm (⅛ in.) diameter wooden dowelling

Two wooden beads about 9 mm (⅜ in.) diameter

Adhesive

To make

Take out the matchbox tray and reinforce it at both short ends by gluing on rectangles of card to fit. In one reinforced end of the tray pierce two holes with the point of the scissors at the positions shown on diagram 7. Make the holes large enough for the lolly sticks to be pushed through. Glue coloured paper to the inside of the base of the tray. Glue trimming round the sides and just over onto the top edge of the tray except for the end with the holes.

Using pattern 19 cut the triangular piece from card. Cover this piece by sticking on a bit of trimming cut to fit as shown in the illustration. Glue the triangular piece in position on the matchbox tray as shown.

For Punch, pare down one end of the lollipop stick to fit into the hole in the wooden head, then stick it in place. Using coloured pens or pencils draw on the facial features as shown in the illustration. For Punch's pointed hat, glue a small piece of ric-rac braid round the head. For his collar thread a guipure flower, or a tiny frill made from lace edging, onto the lolly stick, then glue the collar under the head.

For Punch's costume, glue a piece of 1.3 cm (½ in.) wide ribbon, shawl fashion, around the lollipop stick just below the collar. Turn up one lower corner of the costume and glue it to the front of Punch, enclosing a tiny piece of pared-down matchstick, or cocktail stick, for his baton.

Place Punch in position inside the matchbox tray by pushing the end of the lolly stick through one

of the holes in the end of the tray so that Punch is inside the tray and the end of the stick is outside.

Make Judy in the same way as Punch gluing a piece of guipure trimming or lace to her head for a cap.

For the slide-on cover, take the remaining part of the matchbox and cover it by gluing round a strip of fabric or paper, turning and sticking one raw edge of the fabric to the inside of the matchbox cover at one end. Glue trimming round the opposite end to cover the raw edge of the fabric. Spread glue inside the short edges of the matchbox cover then slide it in place about half way over the matchbox tray as illustrated.

To work the puppets

Hold the box in one hand and push the lollipop sticks up and down, or twist them around, with the other hand.

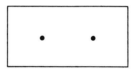

DIAGRAM 7
End of match box tray,
pierce holes at position of dots

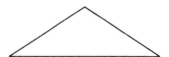

Pattern 19
TRIANGULAR PIECE FOR
TOP OF THE PUPPET SHOW

Left **Figure 47** Punch and Judy puppet show

113

Five fairy tale finger puppets

Figure 48 Five fairy tale finger puppets: princess, queen, witch, king, and prince

These five puppets represent some of the traditional characters to be found in many fairy stories and of course other variations could be made using the same basic puppet idea (fig. 48). They average about 10 cm (4 in.) in height and are easy to make from scraps of fabrics and trimmings. A plain wooden ball or bead is used for each head, and the hands are made from small oval beads, but these can be omitted if desired. If non-fray fabrics are used for the clothes no turnings are required on the raw edges. For other fabrics, turn in the raw edges 3 mm ($\frac{1}{8}$ in.) and glue down.

Materials required

Wooden ball or beads about 18 cm ($\frac{3}{4}$ in.) in diameter
Small oval beads (optional)
Cuttings off nylon tights or stockings
Scraps of fabrics, felt and trimmings
Knitting wool and embroidery thread for the hair
Bits of junk jewellery
Gold or silver paper cut off doyleys etc
Small feathers
A cocktail stick and small bead for the prince's sword
Red pencil and black ball point pen for marking on the facial features
Dried grasses or twigs for the witch's broomstick
Adhesive

To make the basic finger puppet

For the head cut a 4 cm (1$\frac{1}{2}$ in.) diameter circle from double thickness nylon stocking or tights fabric. Place a wooden ball or bead in the centre of the circle, then gather up the edges of the nylon tightly round it. Tie a thread round the gathered nylon to hold the ball or bead in place and form the neck. Trim off the surplus nylon to about 1 cm ($\frac{3}{8}$ in.) away from the tied thread.

For the body cut a 7 cm (2$\frac{3}{4}$ in.) square of fabric. Overlap two opposite edges and stick them together to form a tube that will suit the child's finger. Run a gathering thread round one end of the tube and place it around the gathered nylon at the puppet's neck, pull up the gathers and fasten off then sew the body to the nylon at the neck.

If necessary turn in the lower raw edge and stick, to neaten. Mark the face on each puppet character as shown in the illustration.

The hands should be glued on after the puppet is completed. To make a hand, tie an oval bead inside a small piece of nylon fabric in the same way as for the head. Glue the gathered ends of the hands inside the cape edges then glue the cape fronts to the body.

To make the wicked witch

If available, use green stretchy fabric to cover the head instead of nylon stocking fabric. For the hair cut a few strands of green wool about 7.5 cm (3 in.) long. Glue the strands across the top of the head then tease out the ends with the point of a pin. Stick a bit of black lace to the top of the head to hang down the witch's back.

Cut out the hat using pattern 20a. Slightly overlap and glue the centre back edges. Glue the hat to the head over the lace piece then turn up the lace and stick to the top point of the hat as shown in the illustration.

Cut out the cape using pattern 20b and cutting the lower edge into ragged points as shown on the pattern. Glue the neck edge of the cape around the witch's neck. For the neck frill gather up a scrap of trimming or ribbon and glue it round the neck.

For the broomstick use bits of dried grasses or twigs. Make the handle about 6.5 cm (2$\frac{1}{2}$ in.) long and bind bits of grass to one end with thread. Trim the ends of the grass to an even length. Glue the hands and the broomstick in place as shown in the illustration.

To make the princess

For the hair use twelve strands of embroidery thread to make a plait 13 cm (5 in.) long. Tie a strand of thread round each end of the plait. Glue the centre of the plait to the top of the head then glue the plait down each side of the face.

To the top of the head stick a 4 cm (1$\frac{1}{2}$ in.) diameter circle of net fabric. Make a pointed hat in the same way as for the witch using thin card covered with fabric. Glue the hat to the head then stick a strip of thin transparent fabric to the top point of the hat to hang down the princess's back.

For the cape cut a 7 cm by 9.5 cm (2$\frac{3}{4}$ in. by 3$\frac{3}{4}$ in.) strip of fabric to match the hat trimming. Glue braid to the short edges of the strip then gather one long edge and place it round the neck, pull up the gathers to fit then fasten off. Glue the hand in place and fix a scrap of jewellery round the neck.

To make the queen

For the hair, spread the top, back and sides of the head with glue, then wind a strand of wool round onto the glued area ending at the top of the head.

Make the cape in the same way as for the princess. Make the crown from a strip cut off a doyley formed into a small circle or use braid or trimming. Glue a jewel to the front of the crown. Glue the crown to the

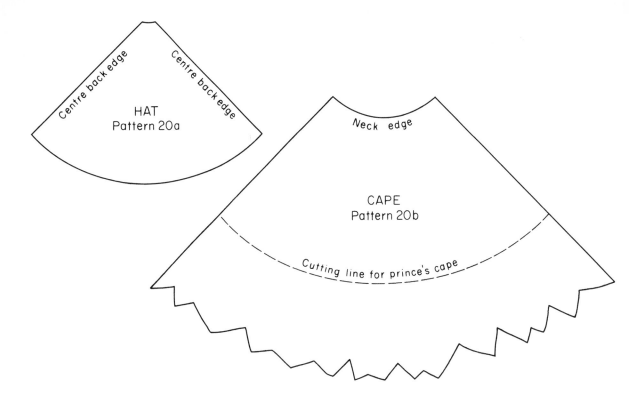

HAT
Pattern 20a

Centre back edge

Centre back edge

Neck edge

CAPE
Pattern 20b

Cutting line for prince's cape

head enclosing the end of a strip of net to hang down the queen's back. Glue the hand in place and glue a bit of chain or string of beads round the neck.

To make the king

For the hair wind a strand of wool about twelve times round three fingers. Pull this small hank of wool off the fingers and glue the centre of the hank to the top of the head then stick the loops in place all round to cover the head. Glue a strip of braid around the body for a belt.

Make the crown, cape, jewellery and the hand in the same way as for the queen.

To make the prince

Make the hair and belt in the same way as for the king. For the hat cut a 4.5 cm (1¾ in.) diameter circle of fabric. Turn the edge of the circle to the wrong side and stick down. Spread glue on the wrong side of the circle except for the turned in edge.

Place the hat on the prince's head pressing and creasing the fabric as necessary to fit. Glue a few feathers to the hat.

Cut out the cape using pattern 20b and cutting the lower edge on the dotted line indicated. Stick trimming to the edges of the cape except for the neck edge, then glue the cape round the neck. Glue a bit of jewellery to the neck of the cape then stick the hand in place.

For the sword cut the cocktail stick to 5 cm (2 in.) in length leaving one end pointed. Glue the small bead to the other end. Cut a bit off the remaining piece of cocktail stick for the cross piece of the sword. Glue it to the sword and also bind it in place with a bit of thread. If desired, paint the sword silver. When dry, glue the sword beneath the left front corner of the cloak.

List of stockists

Great Britain

Most of the materials can be bought from local fabric, ironmonger, handicraft and tobacconist shops or large department stores, or from any of the following firms:

Threads and fabrics

Art Needlework Industries Ltd
7 St Michael's Mansions
Ship Street
Oxford

The Needlewoman Shop
146 Regent Street
London W1

The Felt and Hessian Shop
34 Greville Street
London EC1

Trimmings

Distinctive Trimmings & Co Ltd
11 Marylebone Lane
London W1

Paper and card

Fred Aldous
The Handicrafts Centre
37 Lever Street
Manchester M60 1UX

Paperchase
216 Tottenham Court Road
London W1

Reeves and Sons Ltd
Lincoln Road
Enfield, Middlesex

Kapok and Eclipse magnets

Woolworth's branches

USA

Threads and fabrics

American Crewel Studio
Box 553 Westfield
New Jersey 07091

American Thread Corporation
90 Park Avenue
New York, NY

Appleton Brothers of London
West Main Road
Little Compton
Rhode Island 02837

Craft Yarns
PO Box 385
Pawtucket
Rhode Island 02862

F J Fawcett Co
129 South Street
Boston Massachusetts 02111

Bucky King Embroideries Unlimited
121 South Drive
Pittsburgh
Pennsylvania 15238

Lily Mills
Shelby
North Carolina 28150

The Needle's Point Studio
7013 Duncraig Court
McLean
Virginia 22101

Yarncrafts Limited
3146 M Street
North West
Washington DC

Paper and card

Grumbacher
460 West 34th Street
New York, NY

The Morilla Company Inc
43 21st Street
Long Island City
New York
and
2866 West 7th Street
Los Angeles
California

Strafford-Reeves Inc
626 Greenwich Street
New York
NY 10014

Winsor and Newton Inc
555 Winsor Drive
Secaucus
New Jersey 07094